We Are No Longer at Ease

First published by Jacana Media (Pty) Ltd in 2018

10 Orange Street
Sunnyside
Auckland Park 2092
South Africa
+2711 628 3200
www.jacana.co.za

© Individual contributors, 2018
Cover image © Paballo Thekiso, 2013

All rights reserved.

ISBN 978-1-4314-2678-2

Cover design by Shawn Paikin and Maggie Davey
Design and layout by Lunga Buthelezi
Editing by Lara Jacob
Proofreading by Linda Da Nova
Set in Sabon 11/14pt
Printed by ABC Press, Cape Town
Job no. 003420

See a complete list of Jacana titles at www.jacana.co.za

We Are No Longer at Ease
The Struggle for #FeesMustFall

Edited by
Wandile Ngcaweni and
Busani Ngcaweni

Contents

Acknowledgements ix
Foreword by Malaika wa Azania xi
Introduction by Wandile Ngcaweni and Busani Ngcaweni xv

PART 1: THEORISING THE FEES MUST FALL CAMPAIGN

1. I am so tired *Ntokozo Qwabe* 1
2. Fees Must Fall: A moment in the black radical tradition *Mcebo Freedom Dlamini* 3
3. An open letter to my fellow white UCT students *Jordan Pfotenhauer* 8
4. An end to assimilation, the right to self-determination *Ramabina Mahapa* 11
5. White privilege? But I'm not a racist! *Adam Buch* 15
6. The Fees Must Fall movement and traditional liberation politics in historical perspective: What does it all mean? *Tlhabane Dan Motaung* 17
7. Intellectual openings and policy closures: The many faces of higher education transformation *Busani Ngcaweni and Robert Nkuna* 24
8. The meaning and interpretation of the #FeesMustFall movement: Draft thesis *David Maimela* 29
9. Forgive us Biko for we have betrayed you *Gugu Ndima* . . . 41
10. The ticking time bomb of youth unemployment *Qhama Bona* 47
11. Decolonising where it matters most: TVET colleges *Wandile Ngcaweni* 52
12. The shared lessons of our liberation history: Placing the Congress Youth League in the struggle for #FeesMustFall in South Africa *Asanda Luwaca* 58

13. Why the EFF is gaining ground at South African universities:
    A post #FeesMustFall legacy *Wandile Ngcaweni*...... 68
14. Aryan Kaganof's *Decolonising Wits*: A film analysis
    Azola Dayile 73

PART 2: INTERSECTIONALITY AND FEMINIST PERSPECTIVES

15. Still hungry *Khanyisile Melanie Mboya* 83
16. The University Currently Known as Rhodes:
    Reflections from a female student leader *Khanyisile
    Melanie Mboya*................................. 85
17. #PatriarchyMustFall: Tears, complexities and realisations
    Annabel Fenton................................ 89
18. What solidarity looks like *Sarah Mokwebo* 92
19. 'I Am Stellenbosch' *Nkhensani Manabe*............... 96
20. Student protest gives South Africans a glimpse into
    hidden lives *Sisonke Msimang*.................... 98
21. 'Ignorance is the cure for nothing' *Natasha Ndlebe* 102
22. Power, privilege, hypermasculinity and intersectionality
    Kneo Mokgopa................................ 108
23. When women become a danger to the revolution
    Anele Madonsela................................112

PART 3: WHAT FEES MUST FALL MEANS TO ME

24. What does a revolutionary look like?
    Tshepiso Modupe 121
25. 2015, the year of the student: A personal account
    Rofhiwa Maneta............................... 125
26. Convocation speech at Stellenbosch University – Courage,
    compassion and complexity: Reflections on the new
    Matieland and South Africa *Lovelyn Nwadeyi* 128
27. Black thoughts on white psychology: A student's
    perspective on curriculum transformation
    Kgaugelo Sebidi................................138

28. Sentimentality in remembrance or The born are
    not yet free *Enhle Lucinda Khumalo*............144
29. Many South Africans support #FeesMustFall:
    An open letter to David Maimela
    Busani Ngcaweni............................145
30. The University of Pretoria, DASO and my role as a
    student leader after the 2016 student protests
    Akhona Mdunge..............................150
31. Must we die young? *Nkateko Mabasa*..............156
32. Reflections on #FeesMustFall in the wake of the passing
    of Professor Bongani Mayosi *Sibusiso Chalufu*......160
33. To be a decolonial born again
    Sabelo J. Ndlovu-Gatsheni....................164

PART 4: THE HIGHER EDUCATION POLICY QUAGMIRE

34. University transformation re-imagined: Discourses
    resulting after the Fallist movements
    Mabone Lerato Kgosiemang....................167
35. Young people shook South Africa to the core: Reflections
    of the student protests of 2015 and beyond
    Imraan Buccus..............................175
36. The rise and fall of higher education costs: How 'free'
    is government's free education policy?
    Zuko Godlimpi..............................182
37. Fees Must Fall: A holistic approach will stand us all
    in good stead *Oscar Van Heerden and Nicky Roberts*. 189

Contributors' biographies......................195

Acknowledgements

MANY PEOPLE CONTRIBUTED to the making of this edited volume. We wish to express our sincere gratitude to all the contributors for entrusting us with their work. We also wish to extend our regards to the students and all those who were part of the broad youth movement whose contributions were of pain and sacrifice in pursuit of free, decolonised and quality post-secondary education in South Africa.

In part, this collection of new and revised essays is published as part of the battle of ideas and pays tribute to all those who faced the wrath of police and university authorities in their determination to free poor students from the shackles of unaffordable post-school education. Where articles have appeared in the media before, they are re-published here with the permission of the authors.

We also appreciate assistance and support from friends who encouraged the idea of this especially as it carries the original and authentic voice of student leaders and their supporters in the #RhodesMustFall and #FeesMustFall campaigns.

To our publisher, Neilwe Mashigo, at Jacana Media, thank you. Full credit to Paballo Thekiso, Menzi Mkhize and Wandile Kasibe for supplying images used in this book. Critical comments from peer reviewers are acknowledged.

We are grateful to Yellowwoods Social Investments for their financial support towards publishing this book.

Finally, special thanks to go to Tshepiso Modupe for agreeing to having her picture used on the cover.

Foreword

We revolt simply because, for many reasons, we can no longer breathe.

– Frantz Fanon

THE PAST FIVE YEARS HAVE SHAPED the South African socio-political milieu in ways that are yet to be fully articulated and documented. Not since the apartheid dispensation has the country experienced rapture the magnitude of what it has in the last five years. After what seems like years of resting under the shade of the new democracy, young people of our beloved country decided that they could no longer stay in one place. Somewhere beyond the edges of the tree's shade was a world at war. There was a civilisation that needed to be fashioned. A different South Africa, one that fulfilled the promise of a better life for all, needed to be born. After years of waiting on this new country, the youth realised it was not coming – that they were the ones they had been waiting for. They needed to stand up and step out of the shade, for in their bones they could feel that they were no longer at ease.

It is not an accident of history that young people were at the forefront of the recent struggles. Indeed, the youth has always been instrumental in the struggle for justice, not only in South Africa but throughout the world. In contemporary Africa, the young have made the terrain of struggle their dance floor.

The Y'en a Marre, a Senegalese youth movement, mobilised the youth vote to help oust President Abdoulaye Wade, whose administration had presided over worsening levels of poverty and inequality in the West African nation. The movement continues to be a thorn in the government of Wade's successor, Macky Sall, with it continuously making demands for better reforms. The cascading uprisings in the Middle East and North Africa/Maghreb region (commonly and also problematically referred to as the Arab Spring uprisings) were predominantly led by the youth. The catalyst for these uprisings was the death of Tarek el-Tayeb Mohamed Bouazizi, a Tunisian street vendor who set himself on fire in December 2010. His self-immolation was, at its heart, a demonstration against state sanctioned terror that characterises repressive regimes. Bouazizi was only 26 years old.

The Affirmative Repositioning Movement (ARM) in Namibia, led by young student activist Job Shipululo Amupanda, forced the government into redistributing land to poor working-class youth, who had been systematically thrust at the periphery of economic activity. Amupanda, former secretary for information, publicity and mobilisation of the SWAPO Youth League, was suspended from SWAPO for leading a land occupation campaign in 2014. A year later, a powerful movement that would create a seismic shift in South Africa was born. #RhodesMustFall, the foundation on which the #FeesMustFall movement was built, was born in the corridors of historically white institutions of higher learning.

The movement was a tool of resistance against pervasive institutional racism that defines higher education and, I daresay, the very fibre of South African society. In *Memoirs of a Born Free: Reflections on the Rainbow Nation*, I journey into the lived experiences of many a black working-class child who has to navigate the new South Africa that in some ways is not so new. Though statistics that paint the painful picture of structural inequalities in our country are released annually, they don't sufficiently paint the picture of what racism in all its manifestations does to South Africans. They don't articulate the extent to which it erodes the dignity that should be an inherent right. It is a violent and savage path to which no one should be condemned. Yet, for decades, it has been the experience of many poor working-class students, predominantly black, who have had to fight hard to open the doors of learning and simultaneously rethink and dismantle the legacy of imperialism that is characterised by unjust global hierarchies of knowledge production.

The #RhodesMustFall movement, though often derided by those

who deem its cause capricious, was more than just a struggle about desecrating colonial statues and monuments of colonialism. It was an intellectual struggle that was seeking justice for the epistemological onslaught that African intellectuals and intellectuals in the Global South have been subjected to by the academy that is deeply resistant to change. It situated institutional racism in the broader struggle for transformation and above all, for justice. #FeesMustFall was not different in both substance and form. The struggle for free education has never been simply economic. Since the days of colonial resistance, free education has always meant education that is free to access and that is freed from imperial logic.

On a number of occasions, I have heard some political analysts and commentators refer to the #FeesMustFall protests as spontaneous, implying that they occurred as a result of a sudden impulse, that they were without any stimulus. This characterisation is deeply problematic. It fails to trace the barometer of struggle that led to that historic moment that has, in many ways, shaped the discourse around the depths of the crisis in higher education in South Africa. This struggle cannot be articulated outside a deep understanding of the history of our country, for it is in the womb of imperialism, colonialism and apartheid that the contemporary crisis of higher education gestated.

To paraphrase Elliot-Cooper, geography was a vital component in shaping the imperial ambitions of nation states, but it is also true that imperialism affected more than just the spatiality of colonised nations. It interrupted and, in many ways, annihilated the very ways of life of the colonised people. Godlweska and Smith in their 1994 book *Geography and Empire* contend that this created permanent links between spaces and places that are divided by physicality, but yet are interconnected through ideology and appropriation – the ideology of capitalism that underpins colonialism and apartheid. Even in the democratic dispensation that is seeking to fashion a different society, universities remain a postcolonial microcosm of this devastating legacy. And this is why #FeesMustFall matters.

But to romanticise the #FeesMustFall movement would be a cruel exercise in the rewriting of history; cruel because it would deny the legitimate pain that was suffered by many within the movement. While the movement was progressive in many ways, it also had deep-seated regressive elements that ultimately eroded its revolutionary character. The support-repelling tactics that the movement would later adopt, characterised by the burning of university buildings, the violence targeted at students who did not want to be part of the movement's activities and the aggressive intolerance to dissent were just some of the counter-revolutionary elements that eventually annihilated the moral high-ground that was an important pillar of the movement.

But perhaps the greatest weakness of the movement was the resistance by some of its male leaders to recognise the importance of waging an intersectional struggle. This movement comprised an eclectic blend of people – both in terms of the activists within the movement and those on the outside lending their support – but was often not the safe space that it was supposed to be for women and for the LGBTIQA+ community that in reality was an integral force behind the strength and legitimacy of #FeesMustFall.

I distinctly, and painfully, remember a meeting of #FeesMustFall activists from across the country that was hosted at the Parktonian Hotel in Braamfontein, where the depth of the patriarchal violence within the movement was put on display. A number of male leaders, when confronted about the disregard for the feminist question, boldly spoke about how the struggle was about liberating black people first, and all else would follow. This violent masculinity became a big feature of the movement, attempting, though with constant resistance, to own the narrative of the struggle.

In spite of what became of the movement, it remains important. The struggle for free education matters. We cannot hope to fashion a higher civilisation without attaining this goal. In the words of Arundhati Roy: 'Another world is not only possible, she is on her way. Maybe many of us won't be here to greet her, but on a quiet day, if I listen very carefully, I can hear her breathing.'

Malaika wa Azania, author of *Memoirs of a Born Free: Reflections on the Rainbow Nation* and student at Rhodes University

Introduction

NOW THAT THE 'FEES HAVE FALLEN', systemic challenges of administering fee-free tertiary education notwithstanding, it is time to pause and reflect on the #FeesMustFall campaign, through the voices of those who were at the epicentre of these history-altering student protests. The majority were young men and women who led through formal and informal structures, street protests, graffiti and through writing essays and poems that mobilised students and influenced public opinion. Of course, they faced opposition and support from older members of society. Those voices too are included in this collection in order to balance the perspectives and more importantly, to demonstrate that the recent protests were a continuation of student-led struggles against inequality.

Through this collection of new and, revised articles, we archive the work of some of the thought leaders of the campaign. This should give permanence to the voices of young people in a manner that transcends time and space.

The student protests that heightened in 2015 were a highly emotional episode in the 21st-century history of South Africa, a significant marker of the unease that students felt about the rising costs of tertiary education in the country.

There were many ideas and contestations expressed both on the streets and through writing. Young people put ink to paper to circulate and give perspective on their struggles. The iconography of both the #RhodesMustFall (which preceded protests about fees) and the #FeesMustFall movements symbolised and communicated a clear message: inequality undermines transformation and redress.

The many posters and songs produced created a clear link between dynamics within higher education and the broader political economy of present-day South Africa.

What is noteworthy about the writings that came out of the Fallist movement (a common reference to the students who participated in the #RhodesMustFall and #FeesMustFall protests) was the recognition that the media plays a big role in shaping public opinion. So, the students made effective use of both traditional (newspapers) and new (electronic) media to champion their cause. As some commentators often noted, the leadership of these movements were broad and voices were diverse while still pursuing a common decolonisation purpose.

In this book, we capture the voices of the student movements as part of our humble contribution to the archive. As already stated, this collection aims to bring the voiceless or those who otherwise might simply be dismissed as agent provocateurs to the mainstream. It adds to other efforts by young writers and established scholars doing research and writing projects on the same subject.

We Are No Longer at Ease is a collection of articles and essays that tell the story from both personal and political perspectives. We have reflections from radical feminist voices in this edition. Furthermore, it was necessary to include ongoing policy debates on higher education in South Africa. The essays are primarily from young people across the racial lines, who took part in the movement. Most reflect the diversity and somewhat 'blurred' political allegiances that existed in the movement. It is important to respect and document these various opinions and experiences without bias and interpretation because through them we learn how activists felt and dealt with differences during the course of the movements. The voices expressed in this book are from various universities across the country. Furthermore, this collection embraces different forms of expression and writing styles in a manner that brings authenticity to the stories being told.

Hence the reader will find a range of pieces – poems, academic essays and articles. Few of them have been previously published but most of these have been updated with new introductions. These were important to include in the collections to build the archive and show that students were indeed involved in thinking about issues and were active in informing and educating broader society about their struggles. In fact, it is our view that these articles shaped public opinion and mobilised society to rally behind the students' efforts. As a result, the decolonisation call resonated across the colour and class lines, beyond campus caucuses into political parties from various ideological tendencies.

We also felt it necessary to include pieces by young intellectuals and/or political commentators who were themselves student leaders during their time in different institutions prior to 2015, because the movements' foundations were laid by former generations of students who also fought similar battles.

Therefore, this collection includes works of young student leaders turned academic and public commentators; student newspaper journalists that were covering the protests; public commentators who aimed to inform the broader South African society about distinct aspects of the movement; scholars who helped students articulate and find clarity in the way they voiced their ideas on decolonisation; foot soldiers on the ground leading students through the police brutality of rubber bullets and pepper spray; and, most importantly, voices of younger students who are still at university, agitating for results and fulfilment of promises made during and following the student protests of 2015.

Why no longer at ease?
The title of the book, *We Are No Longer at Ease: The Struggle for #FeesMustFall*, is meant to provoke thoughts and feelings about what the movement was, what it stood for and to whom it belonged. The movement was a contested space; there was a continuous battle for hegemony of ideas – political, philosophical and otherwise. On the other hand, there was contestation wherein the university administrators wanted to control and shape the direction of the movement but the students were putting pressure on them to ensure that they, as owners of the movement, as most of them believed, decided on the direction the movement would take. They refused to be told how to protest. They refused to accept that changes would come gradually. Most importantly, the iconography and songs of the movement tell stories of young people who are no longer at ease; to paraphrase Chinua Achebe, a generation refusing to co-exist with inequality.

The title also seeks to capture the continuous nature of the nervous condition of being black, young and never at ease in South Africa. The results and legacy of the student movement can arguably be traced to have begun in December 2017 in two extremes, the first being the announcement of free education by President Zuma, which has received applause by students, and the second being the conviction of Khanya Cekeshe and Bonginkosi Khanyile, which has received harsh criticism. The continuous pursuit by the state of students who were arrested and charged for their actions, or lack thereof, during the student's protests has been called deplorable by students who believe they are still being victimised for protesting for a just cause. It is unlikely that the on-going cases against students who participated are going to be dropped by the state and the universities. Other students and prominent leaders of the protests like Mcebo Dlamini, who finds voice in this book, are still being pursued. In many ways because of this developing deplorable legacy of the student movement, it is clear that the struggle for fees has not been complete and will most likely continue for years and perhaps even a lifetime for individuals like Khanya Cekeshe, Bonginkosi Khanyile and many others who pay a high personal price for the attainment of free education.

How the book is organised

We Are No Longer at Ease is divided into four thematic sections namely, Theorising the Fees Must Fall Campaign; Intersectionality and Feminist Perspectives; What Fees Must Fall Means to Me; and The Higher Education Policy Quagmire.

Part 1: Theorising the Fees Must Fall Campaign deals with philosophical and political ideas. The politics of ideas were the reason for the spark of protests in 2015 when students decided to question the entire idea of the university in South Africa. There was an attempt to merge ideas and the politics of protest as a seamless movement. Politics in South Africa has always been driven by contestation of ideas and philosophies. The student protest for instance was a space contested by those who lean on Black Consciousness, Pan-Africanist, African Nationalist traditions etc. All these ideals had to find space to express themselves but there were also ideas that dominated for the first time such as intersectionality, in many ways further displacing hopes to remember and re-centre ideas of certain personalities that had been perceived as forgotten and marginalised at the time of the movement.

It is also particularly important to engage with these ideas after the protests, failures and successes of the movement notwithstanding.

All revolutions have political roots from which they bloom, and some who shaped those political ideas during the movements, such as Ntokozo Qwabe, Mcebo Dlamini and Ramabina Mahapa, find their work presented in this book.

Part 2: Intersectionality and Feminist Perspectives contains some of the most important ideas and discourses to emerge from and during the movement. The student protests revealed many complexities of gender inequality that exists in broader society in South Africa. Some may argue that the chasm that emerged between the genders was a revelation, that after 1994 many attitudes and norms persisted unchecked – patriarchy and misogyny being the sharpest thorns. It proved true during the protests that women and gender non-binary individuals suffer a worse fate in this country, with the triple burden of being black, women, gender queer and poor. The conversation on patriarchy shone its ugly face in the student protests when allegations of misogyny, rape and homophobia emerged. These abuses did not, however, go unchallenged as the essays in this section will demonstrate. Conversations on intersectionality gained momentum. Those who drove these conversations about the toxicity of patriarchy called out the misogynistic nature of the student movement and demanded that there be space for voices to represent the agency of non-masculine persons too.

It is important that we highlight that gender politics was a significant and important part of the movement. The chapters in this section are evidence of women's voices leading, writing and making sense of their role and place in the movement. It is also evidence of a young group of women leading society in conversation and thought on matters it had not confronted. Authors like Khanyisile Melanie Mboya, Anele Madonsela as well as Annabel Fenton give an intimate account of their experience as women in the movement. Sarah Mokwebo, Kneo Mokgopa reveal that perhaps one of the biggest mistakes of the movement was rejecting intersectionality, thus openly inviting patriarchy to thrive. Much is still to be documented and written by women on the role they played and continue playing after the student protests, but we hope this will contribute positively to that body of work.

Part 3: What Fees Must Fall Means to Me delves into the intimate and personal experiences of individuals, some of whom led on the ground and literally put their bodies in the firing line. These essays reveal details of the psychological toll that participating in the movement took on the students. Enhle Khumalo and Lovelyn Nwadeyi were some such students.

Part 4: The Higher Education Policy Quagmire deals with policy debates, which are important in mapping a way forward. The main reasons for these protests was because higher education had failed over the many years of democracy to formulate necessary policy. Other debates on policy bring in the governing party, the African National Congress (ANC), to deplore how it failed to action their own party policies and implement them in government. The ANC has admitted their failure in this regard, but they have also strangely congratulated themselves as victors of the student protests as they believe themselves to have granted fee-free education for the poor. Authors Imraan Buccus and Zuko Godlimpi give much-needed insight on this debate.

Conclusion

It was impossible to cover all aspects of the protests in this one volume because of the range and scope of issues at hand. Many other topics are not covered in this archive, but we hope what it is successful in doing is contributing positively to society's knowledge of the students' movement of 2015 and beyond. We are confident that it will uniquely enrich the archive that may already exist about the movement.

We hope it will be successful in making all who read it, especially students who were part of and those who will be part of higher education institutions of South Africa in the future, reflect on the movement. Most importantly, we hope *We Are No Longer at Ease* will rekindle the debate around the nature and causes of student protests in South Africa.

Young people are not at ease. They are refusing to co-exist with coloniality, sexism, democratic indifference and inequality. We need to acknowledge and take heed of their calls.

PART I
THEORISING THE FEES MUST FALL CAMPAIGN

I am so tired

Ntokozo Qwabe

I AM SO TIRED.
I am tired of white people and their tears.
I am tired of white people not getting it and not being interested in getting it.
I am tired of white people thinking they have the legitimacy to speak over us, 'debate' us over and 'disagree' with us about issues which are NOT about them, which they are not systematically affected by, which they know little about.
I am tired of white people making themselves the centre of our existence.

I am so so tired.
I am tired of white people centralising themselves in conversations about us.
I am tired of white people and their white 'scholarly communities' that tokenise and disrespect us.
I am tired of white people pretending to love us when their actions fuck us over all the damn time.
I am tired of 'progressive' white liberals who spend time trying to save us when the white community needs the most saving.
I am tired of white liberals whose 'activism' is for woke points and an eternal shield from their own white supremacy ever being problematised/engaged with.
I am tired of white liberals who want us to 'teach' them what to do.

I am so so tired.
I am tired of white 'scholarly communities' who gag us into being okay with the veneration of murderous, black-bloodthirsty, white supremacist bastards whose crimes enabled these communities to exist.
I am tired of our erased voices, labour and blood forever serving the ends of white supremacy.
I am tired of white people messing up and drowning us in their white tears when we call them out.
I am tired of forever having to assert my humanity and the dignity of my people.
I am tired because I can no longer breathe.
I am so so done with all this bullshit.

Fees Must Fall: A moment in the black radical tradition

Mcebo Freedom Dlamini

What am I? A question that I should not have asked myself. I am trapped here, and I am screaming, if you can hear me please respond. I am calling for help. The labyrinth is more complicated than I had imagined, and I am in the middle of it. Forward is evasive and backward is a mirage. I have no other choice but to continue the fight or die.

— Mbe Mbhele

HOW DOES ONE BEGIN TO THINK of beauty in a place that remembers nothing except ruin? To speak about blackness or anything that implicates it is a difficult task and to do so often is to speak truth to power and once done it cannot be undone. The Fees Must Fall (FMF) movement was a moment in blackness. How does one give an account of such a complex moment that not only bears the screams of the present but carries cries of generations before and after us? Here I will attempt to say certain things about the movement. These will not be conclusive, but it is the inconclusiveness of these things that will allow us to continue to think further about the labyrinth that is the FMF movement.

Black students were chanting and the police started shooting. Students began running, but the police continued shooting. Students hid behind walls and some beneath tables, but the popping sound of the gun was relentless. This cycle continued for days, weeks, months; some say it has been going on for centuries. Black people have always been confronted with violence. It is in fact this violence that makes them black. It is enough for us to be black. I give this background to try and highlight the fact that the FMF movement was part of a tradition of black resistance. It is important for us to locate FMF within this tradition such that we do not run the risk of erasing certain contributions that other black people have made in the struggle. It is almost impossible to think about FMF outside the spirit of the June 1976 protests in the same way that the 1976 protests are unimaginable outside of the Sharpeville massacre or the Women's March to the Union Buildings. All these moments are connected and FMF is a continuation of the fight for complete liberation of black people in Africa and in the diaspora. The FMF movement was hugely inspired by the Rhodes Must Fall movement (RMF) which started a couple of months prior to the FMF movement.

RMF not only gave FMF language to articulate some of its demands but it also played an important role in influencing the radical praxis of FMF. This is to say that the RMF movement was important theoretically as well as practically. It is important that this detail be mentioned because FMF and RMF became one even though they were not conceived as such, with some even arguing that the movements were formed for different reasons. The formation of the movement was not in isolation because these movements are part of a history of resistance by a people who know no life outside of subjugation and oppression.

To paraphrase Fred Moten, FMF was testament to the fact that objects (dehumanised people) do and have throughout history been resisting.

Black students were fighting against the increase of university fees. Black students were dying for university fees to fall. Others were shouting words like 'Land' and 'Dignity'. Students carried placards written 'Decolonisation Now'.

The media reported that the students do not have an idea of what they are fighting for or against. Some reported that they were fighting because they were too lazy to study. Almost everyone had an opinion on why the students were chanting and singing. Others came with recommendations on how the students should be fighting. Some joined the students. Other students eventually became fatigued and they stopped waking up in the morning to go to the protests. Younger students joined in. But the movement continued even when the media stopped reporting. Universities became spaces of protest. Workers became students and students became workers. We became black. Is that not that a beautiful thing? Our blackness became our source of unity.

We were no longer just fighting against an increment of fees. We were fighting against all ills that affected black people in our society. In our unconscious we knew very well that when we say Fees Must Fall we are actually saying blacks and all other oppressed groups must rise. We understood that the fees question could not be separated with that of land because in actual fact accommodation in universities is more costly than tuition. We understood that even if every academically deserving black person were to go to university our universities would be saturated because there aren't enough universities in South Africa.

We were fully aware of all these limitations but we were actually saying that all forms of oppression against the black man must be dismantled. This is what many people who saw themselves as intellectuals could not appreciate. They analysed the movement literally failing to read its nuance.

Women started caucusing and men started noticing. We started seeing sjamboks. The police continued shooting. The popping sound of the gun was unwavering. It is Pumla Gqola who says that our lives are always imbued in contradictions. This was true even in the movement; the gender question became one that we could no longer ignore. I write about it here with full knowledge of the fact that what I say might be coming from the place of patriarchal privilege and therefore not completely accurate. This is one of the lessons we learned through the movement. That for a long time in black resistance movements the voice of women has always been erased or dwarfed to that of a supporting role. The women who were part of the FMF were hell bent on ensuring that this continuum in history is interrupted. Upon seeing that the movement was toxic because of hypermasculinity, women decided to speak up and create a hashtag within a hashtag. They formed a group called #ImbokodoMustLead. The group, through the use of symbolism, raised questions around leadership, rape, sexual violation and other gender-related ills that existed in the movement. It is at this point that they said, 'The revolution will be black and intersectional'. Here they revealed to us, see, that even though our blackness was what we all had in common there were other stratifications within us that could not be ignored. They showed that the class and gender question is important in how we articulate our demands. They showed that none of these categories were more important than the other. It is for this that the intervention of black women in FMF is an important one in the history of black resistance.

Films were created about the incidents and books were written. Leaders were created and the masses accepted their status. They sang praises, wrote poems and painted murals. Leaders got arrested and the masses showered them with more love. They appeared in magazines and were attending conferences around the world. A few whispered their discomfort about how their leaders had changed. Nothing changed, the police did their thing and less people went to the protests. Power does corrupt, maybe not absolutely, but it does have the potential of destroying organisations. With the FMF gaining popularity not only in South Africa but around the world, more people wanted to fund the movement. We needed people to organise those funds. We needed to decide who would go to the conferences and dinners. We needed to start operating in an organised manner. This caused many fractures within the movement because everyone wanted to have their hands on the pie.

People came from nowhere to dictate how the movement must operate. This became a major stumbling block in the growth of the organisation because instead of discussing ideas and issues, we were having debates on logistics and leadership. This was not the only problem. Our respective political parties also deepened the cracks that existed. Since the movement attracted and accepted people from different organisations, those inherent antagonisms that existed previously between those organisations found expression in the movement.

The Economic Freedom Front (EFF) found the ruling African National Congress (ANC) lacking in not being radical enough and failing to deliver free education, even after being in power for 20 years. The ANC countered this attack on them by saying that the EFF was being opportunistic and that it was using the movement to attract followers by making populist statements. As those in the forefront, we received calls from the leaders of our political parties dictating to us what we ought to do. This affected our morale not only as leaders but even as members of the movement. There were others who were given money to destabilise and cause confusion within the movement, which leads us to think carefully about the role that political parties have played either in derailing the struggle or advancing it.

I am generally sceptical about the role of political parties but in the absence of effective alternatives, one accepts them and tries to navigate through the difficulties.

Many educated people felt that the students were wasting their time and that they would fail. But it was not only the students who were protesting; workers also joined and there was general public sympathy for the student struggles. It is well documented that at institutions like UNISA and the University of Johannesburg, FMF protests were soon followed by calls for insourcing. This led to contract workers being fully employed in these universities. The movement was no longer a student movement. Communities started contributing to the movement. For example, there was an instance at Wits university where members of the public organised and delivered food to protesting students as part of the pledge for solidarity.

When the movement was at its peak, the number of other protests making genuine demands increased. Learners in high schools voiced their opinion against all laws and practices that sought to make their identities inferior. For example, provinces like Gauteng recorded protests by the Congress of South African Students (COSAS) who also pledged solidarity with their university counterparts.

It is also a well-publicised fact that many universities in South Africa have set up structures tasked with the responsibility of making changes to their curriculum, thanks to the influence of students who called for decolonisation of higher education.

No one can deny the influence of FMF in bringing forth the debate around land and race in South Africa. This being said, there is still a long way to go in order for us to unshackle ourselves from the chains of oppression. The spirit of FMF must continue to live on and inspire us to continue with the fight.

An open letter to my fellow white UCT students

Jordan Pfotenhauer

I THINK IT IS NECESSARY TO OPEN with a few disclaimers. Firstly, please do not respond to this with comments like 'not all white people...' That is not the point and not what I am trying to convey here. Your persecution complex is unbecoming. Secondly, I am not a hypocrite. I'm aware that I have done many of the things I criticise in this article. This is a letter to myself just as much as it is to all of you. Finally, I do not intend to speak on behalf of people of colour in this article. If that is the tone in which this piece comes across, I apologise deeply. I have tried my best for that not to be the case.

The other day, while listening to some SRC candidates deliver their manifestos, I noticed something that troubled me but which I have come to expect. In response to a candidate speaking passionately about racial issues and her experience as a black person at UCT, several white students looked very uncomfortable. I knew why. To us, talking about race in such an open way is 'outdated', something taboo in the 'New South Africa'.

[Fun game: Watch a white person trying to describe the difference between two individuals, when their only real distinguishing factor is their race. 'Um, they were both women ... and tall... One was wearing a hat, I think?']

Race has become a no-go topic to white people. At a cursory glance, this seems marvellous because, in our society, to be colour-blind is to be a prejudice-free saint. This is wrong. To be colour-blind is to be ignorant. Sorry to the white person who 'really does not see race at all' and who expects my envy and adoration because of this. I'm calling your bluff.

What you don't realise is that when you say, 'race doesn't matter' or 'I wish people would stop being so racial', you're oversimplifying an issue that desperately needs discussing. (Also, if a white person could explain to me what 'being racial' even means – that would be pleasant, thanks.)

When you accuse someone of 'playing the race card' when they attempt to discuss their oppression, you're being an active agent in the said oppression. And when you commit the worst transgression of the lot, and try to tell me, 'Apartheid is over. We need to move on', I want to cry because apartheid may be over but racial inequality sure as hell is not.

Moreover, as a white person it is a lot easier for you to say things like that. It is easy to say race does not matter when your race is the one dominant in the media. It is easy to say race does not matter when the statue that is arguably the centrepiece of Upper Campus doesn't commemorate and celebrate someone who oppressed your people for decades.

It's easy to say race doesn't matter when a significant factor in your parents' success was the fact that they were white under apartheid. This is something white people really do not like admitting. I am not saying your parents didn't work hard. However, if they had had dark skin and they worked just as hard, they would not be nearly as successful.

But it is not about race anymore though, is it? It is about class now, you protest. That may be true, but how many black people went to your swanky high school? How many white people live in Khayelitsha? In South Africa, race is class, certainly in the vast majority of cases. The more we ignore that fact, the more idiotic we look. In doing so, we also ignore the fact that the rich black UCT student still suffers. She is still put in a box synonymous with her race. Her achievements, no matter how deserved, are always scrutinised with doubt. 'Did she make it to UCT because she's smart?' people ask, 'or is she just another lazy freeloader, benefiting from an admissions policy that keeps our deserving white friends out and puts people like her in their place?'

[The careful reader will notice the lack of any racial identifiers in this accusation. That is the point I am trying to make. You don't have to say 'black' for something to be racist, and not saying it usually compounds the problem.]

The unfortunate reality is that because a white guy is writing this it's probably going to gain a lot more traction than if a person of colour did. That's because if a black person were to write this, they would be put in a box. The box would be given an inescapable label, something like 'angry, bitter black person', and statements like the ones previously mentioned would be thrown at it. As a white person writing this, I am like a Woolworths meal to you. Palatable.

That being said, you are probably feeling quite attacked right now. This is good. If that's what it takes for you to finally become cognizant of your privilege, then that is great.

But what now? Well, the bad news is that you can't change the fact that you have privilege. What you can do, however, is use that privilege advantageously. Speak out when a white friend says something racist. Be constantly vigilant of your inner biases. Only when we realise that racism is a living, breathing monster within us can we actually start to fight it.

We need to start discussing race without euphemisms, without ignorance and without sugar-coating the difficult issues. Denying that it is a complex, multifaceted issue does nobody any favours, least of all ourselves.

First published on bonfire.com, 22 September 2014, http://www.bonfiire.com/cape-town/2014/09/an-open-letter-to-my-fellow-white-uct-students-or-why-is-black-a-swearword-to-white-south-africans/

An end to assimilation, the right to self-determination

Ramabina Mahapa

While the #FeesMustFall movement has made an enormous contribution towards advancing the struggle for free education in South Africa, it failed to consolidate its support and sustainably organise itself to continue the difficult task of bringing about a decolonised education system. Given that power concedes only when given no other alternative, there is a need to organise students nationally towards building a non-partisan student political formation that will secure the #FeesMustFall gains and further carry the baton for free decolonised education forward. The speech below, directed at UCT's black alumni, sought to challenge the assertion dominant within our society at the time that black people's problems emanate primarily from the ANC-led government. The speech sought to remind black people, especially at UCT, of what we ought to understand as our chief problem.

As I was thinking about what to say tonight, I came to a realisation that I need to focus on part of the cause of the black man's plight and not the symptoms. And I want to have a frank discussion.

We find ourselves at a time at UCT where students are no longer complaining and sitting down on their buttocks talking of transformation. Students have risen up and taken the hefty burden of bringing about radical and progressive change to the institution. Martin Luther King Jr once said that 'the hottest place in hell is reserved for those who remain neutral in times of great moral conflict'.

The students have decided to speak out. What about yourselves?

Are you going to commence with your life's quest to maximise utility as a consumer and economic profit as a producer? Are you willing to sacrifice your privilege and join the clarion call evoked by students and stand with us in saying 'no more, we cannot breathe in this space'? Whites continue to use their positions of privilege to create a socio-political quagmire such that the blacks fight among themselves. The new generation has been bamboozled into believing that the government, led by the African National Congress, is the problem.

Undeniably, the ANC is liable for some of the challenges facing the black masses. But the black people's problem is still chiefly the potency of whiteness. In the new democratic dispensation, we have only been concerned with the 'rainbow nation' rhetoric and singing 'kumbaya' while our economy still reflects the same socio-economic disparities of the apartheid era. Democracy has granted a few blacks seats at the master's table; the rest are still fighting over breadcrumbs falling off the table. And it is these few and mostly politically connected 'privileged' blacks who assist their white masters in maintaining the status quo.

Whites have not even begun to see blacks as equals and as being capable of thinking for themselves. They continually want to have a say in how we break the shackles of oppression administered and maintained by them. They cry foul as soon as blacks start organising and speaking for themselves. Deep down they understand that they stand to lose their privileges. The white liberal has continued to play a rather peculiar role in the oppression of the black masses, his racist and conservative ways continue to be shielded in his subtle and 'angelic' approach. It is the white liberal who is at the forefront of spreading the gospel of integration and a peaceful society. White liberals point towards white conservatives as the problem and they have convinced themselves that they have arrived at enlightenment pertaining to the sins committed by their forefathers. Yet subconsciously, they share the same set of values and desire to protect their privileges.

The ideology and culture of formerly 'whites only' spaces has still not changed. What has taken place is that blacks can now access those spaces of learning and living in order to immerse themselves in a Western culture. Thus, for the blacks to enjoy the benefits of accessing those places they have to integrate into whiteness. Our integration is nothing but black people assimilating to what is still regarded as righteous, ordained, intelligent, beautiful and angelic whiteness.

It is a matter of fact that integration has benefited whites as opposed to blacks. Those blacks that now sit at the same table with whites have had to rid themselves of their languages, cultures and overall sense of self, and so have lost more than they will ever gain.

The so-called integration in South Africa has given blacks a false sense of hope and belonging that leads them to misdiagnose the cause of their plight. It cannot be the case that even to this day blacks are still seen as mere appendages to a white society. How is it that we have become content with a university like UCT that has six permanent, full-time African professors and only five permanent, full-time coloured professors? Xolela Mangcu wrote that the number of black South African academic staff at UCT in 2013 was 48 out of a total of 1 405, which is only 3%.

How can we remain content with such statistics? Our present-day society, deeply rooted in capitalist values and ideals, is characterised by gross poverty, deaths from preventable diseases, corruption and starvation. We have machinery that gives abundance and a rich earth that provides abundantly, but many are still in need. More than intelligence, we need compassion, love and humanity.

Our path leads only to despondency and destitution; is dystopia the end we seek? May the hour come upon us where we suspend our egoistic attitudes and dedicate ourselves to eradicating poverty and inequality. We have got to realign our ends to a commitment to a better life for all.

Freedom is not having the opportunity to be white or to live like whites. It is the right to self-determination and a dignified life.

It must be known that what is taking place is only the beginning. Blacks must fathom the fact that whites still remain in positions of power. We therefore need to consolidate our power and break the resistance of the white community in trying to preserve the status quo. Blacks need to rally behind dismantling white supremacy to its very core.

It is always us blacks wanting to reconcile, to forgive and forget, while white folks stand on the sidelines, enjoying their privilege. No matter how much flowery language you may employ to conceal the truth, the reality is that it is the whites who have reaped the benefits of our negotiated democracy, while blacks have gotten a raw deal. We are murdered in plain daylight for demanding a decent living wage from white capitalists and nothing is done about it.

It is saddening to see institutions of higher learning, like UCT, being the hub of massive creation of non-whites (blacks who worship at the altar of whiteness). UCT's environment propagates Uncle Toms (i.e. black subservients) who will take every opportunity to ridicule blacks who speak of the problem of racism; they claim that class is the issue. The majority of our people are not fooled by this façade of lies; our struggle is not simply class antagonisms. Liberal institutions are the factories that offer blacks who aspire to be white, despite their pigmentation, an opportunity to do so.

Blacks are being enticed with very little, like a carrot being dangled in front of a donkey – with the perception of change in sight, yet never reaching the end result. Black folks must rid themselves of the ulcer called assimilation. We need to eliminate the need to assimilate in any way, shape or form to whiteness because we are perpetuating our own oppression and the destruction of our humanity. Unity amongst blacks is a necessary first step and the goal is self-determination towards the creation of an independent African society.

Statement delivered at the UCT Association of Black Alumni discussion on transformation, 9 April 2015. Available at: https://www.news.uct.ac.za/article/-2015-04-09-an-end-to-assimilation-the-right-to-self-determination

White privilege? But, I'm not a racist!
Adam Buch

AN ALARMING BUT COMMON RESPONSE to the issues of institutional racism and white privilege is the inevitable 'white defence': 'But, I am not a racist!', or something to that effect. This is not a defence – there should be no defence in the first place.

Now that the statue of Rhodes has been removed, we must begin preparing for the immense work that still needs to be done. Beyond symbols and names, we need to look at discourses, institutions and structures. The bigger picture. This entails engaging with the broader concerns regarding systematic and institutional racialism (and, unfortunately, racism). Enter white privilege.

White privilege as a concept and experience – and, in some instances, a judgement – is one that is met with fear and disengagement. As many of you reading this will have heard, the 'but, I'm not a racist' defence has become a common part of the dialogue – if you can call it that.

I am a white, heterosexual male and, in many instances, I have been considered 'the enemy'. Now, I take issue with that title on me, but if someone calls me out on being privileged as a white man, I accept it. I do not want it. I do not support it. I wish I could change it. But I am part of white privilege. As are all white South Africans.

In my engagements on campus surrounding the issues of symbolism, heritage and cultural monopolies, it has come to light that white privilege has been paralleled with racism towards black South Africans. This is not completely the case. Those who consider themselves non-racist are not part of the discourse but fail to understand that being a South African and understanding its historical narrative means that one is already part of the racial discourses in this country.

When black South Africans experience institutional racism, then we, as white South Africans, need to recognise our part in this discourse and our white privilege. There cannot be institutional racism without institutional privilege. There cannot be disadvantage without advantage somewhere else.

White South Africans should not take the suggestion of white privilege as an attack. It is an observation and an experience that requires engagement and understanding. This is addressed to those white South Africans that use the 'but, I'm not a racist' defence. You do not have to agree with the exclusivity of privilege or consider superiority to be privileged. These structures exist and we, as South Africans, are part of them.

Rather than defending yourself against the idea of racism, open up to the structures and institutions in place independent of yourself. Listen, talk and engage in this discourse and start a dialogue. Be part of the transformation that this institution (UCT) and South Africa at large so desperately needs.

Personally, I revel in the opportunity to break free of white privilege and the opportunity to engage with the abhorrent experiences of those who are disenfranchised by institutional racism. Being a South African – white or black – means that you are part of the discourse of race. Only by accepting this and engaging can we begin to reconcile and, hopefully, start the transformation that this country has not seen enough of in the past 24 years of democracy.

Like the removal of the Cecil John Rhodes statue, acknowledging and, indeed, accepting white privilege is a step in the right direction. Ending the glorification of white liberalism and the national apathy towards genuine, meaningful and lasting transformation begins with our engagement in the discourses around us, not hiding from them.

First appeared in Varsity, 74(4): 5, 14 April 2015, *http://varsitynewspaper.co.za/ opinions/4026-white-privilege-im-not-racist*

The Fees Must Fall movement and traditional liberation politics in historical perspective: What does it all mean?

Tlhabane Dan Motaung

Personal background

I SERVED AS THE DEPUTY GENERAL SECRETARY of the South African Student Congress (SASCO), Wits University branch in 1995 and its branch general secretary in 1996. This time was characterised by a strong intellectual climate within the ranks, with political discussion papers either commissioned or voluntarily drafted from time to time, but especially in the build up to the elective conference, at both branch and national levels. SASCO debated its ideological orientation and, at least at Wits branch level, cast itself into the socialist mould. Most of the SASCO leaders and members were members of the African National Congress (ANC) and the Mass Democratic Movement at large.

It is safe to say SASCO saw its role on campuses as being the furtherance of the aims and objectives of the National Democratic Revolution (NDR), the ANC political theory covering both the approach to the anti-apartheid struggle and the post-apartheid vision. SASCO's struggles reflected the inchoate state of the newly democratised South Africa, with much of the historical disabilities, material and non-material, visibly in place, not least in terms of the university experience of black students.

Twenty-three years after my involvement in student activism, my academic transcript is still endorsed with the words 'certificate of character withdrawn', which means that what I did at Wits then remains permanent and therefore I am unable to register in any other university in South Africa. Over two decades with a negative academic transcript is probably longer than a criminal record.

Introduction

There is no denying that the Fees Must Fall movement was a consciousness-altering, transformative, historical force that shook up the very foundations of our assumptions about South African post-apartheid politics. However, the Fees Must Fall movement neither emerged nor unfolded within the hegemonic philosophical camp of the African National Congress (ANC) revolutionary politics and ideological leadership nor any traditional liberation politics. From its very beginnings, the Fees Must Fall movement defined itself in antithetical terms to the status quo, openly calling for the dismemberment of both the tangible and intangible manifestations of all perceived manifestations of Eurocentrism in South Africa. At the same time, this student movement expanded its philosophical canvas to embrace all historically marginalised social forces. This essay seeks to account for this phenomenon, by advancing the thesis that the Fees Must Fall Movement broadly represents continuity with the historical struggle for transformation insofar as the racially defined socio-economic inequalities have largely remained transgenerationally immutable in society, not least in the education area. On the other hand, the Fees Must Fall movement must be seen as a rupture, a break with the brand of liberation struggle politics that fought apartheid forces. Politically and philosophically, the emergence of the Fees Must Fall movement poses a central question about the adequacy of traditional liberation politics in the historical task of transforming society in the post-apartheid era.

This rupture is emphasised by the fact that the Fees Must Fall movement arose despite the virtual monopoly of the ANC-aligned South African Student Congress (SACSO) in student politics on university campuses across the country, because SASCO was widely seen as being an integral part of the broader Mass Democratic Movement historically spearheaded by the ANC. The position of this essay is that the Fees Must Fall movement signals a fundamental shift in post-apartheid revolutionary politics. The movement must be understood as crucial to the possibilities for alternative progressive politics at a time when the ANC's historical influence on society is noticeably on the wane as the party succumbs to the allurement of post-colonial power politics in what has been generally termed 'the sins of incumbency'.

What sets the Fees Must Fall movement apart from anything seen before in post-apartheid student politics was its insistence on linking students' socio-political experience with the wider national political landscape, transcending sectarian differences as it questioned the very credentials of the national political legitimacy underpinning post-apartheid society. Furthermore, for the first time in the post-apartheid era, South Africa saw the appearance of a political discourse, or lingua franca, that went beyond the standard repertoire that had until then defined the spirit of the age. The Fees Must Fall movement therefore was a clear departure both in form and content from what had been understood to be the language of South African politics.

The Fees Must Fall movement was an expressly non-partisan student movement. The fact that it shunned ideological alignment with any of the existing political parties could be ascribed to it finding revolutionary politics inadequate to addressing the challenges facing South Africa in the current historical period. It is not hard to see the causal link between the Fees Must Fall movement in South Africa and the Arab Spring in the Middle East as well as Black Lives Matter in America, and other global, youth-led movements that question power structures, establishment politics and the status-quo-maintaining leadership claims of historically leftist politics. At a more significant level, the emergence of the Fees Must Fall movement points to a lacuna in the intellectual, political and historical discourse championed by the liberation movement as the progressive agenda in South Africa. Any attempt at understanding not only the emergence of the movement but its defining character as a force outside the traditional revolutionary politics of South Africa should lead to both the realisation and the conclusion that the last decade has seen some drastic decline in the historical legitimacy of the ANC as a liberation movement enjoying political currency in the eyes of broader society.

The decade under the political leadership of President Thabo Mbeki saw the increasing fortunes of the ANC on all fronts. However, these gains were not made ex nihilo. An argument could be made that the virtual predominance of the ANC during this period was tied to the intellectual leadership provided by President Mbeki, who had established himself as one of the premiere Africanist thinkers within the ANC. His 'I am an African' speech, delivered during the adoption of the South African constitution in 1996, not only lifted the nation to a higher level of self-consciousness as an emergent African nation, but at once disarmed and pre-empted any political and intellectual force that could have bypassed the ANC on its Africanist credentials. Thabo Mbeki's intellectual leadership and political innovation on the African continent can thus be seen as contributing to the incubatory climate that led to the emergence of the Fees Must Fall movement, at least in the long term, given his foundational call to African cultural and intellectual regeneration. His emphatic Africanist credentials thus assured the ANC hegemony as the undisputed representative of the progressive, transformative, African-centric agenda.

The Zuma era unravelled this process considerably and tragically reduced the ANC to the stereotypical African postcolonial liberation movement that fails ordinary Africans, especially the working and underclasses as well as peasants. At the level of public discourse, the Zuma-led ANC degenerated to name-calling and delegitimising opponents with such labels as 'clever blacks', 'counter-revolutionary' and 'Western agent' lavishly sprinkled in the public domain. Consequently, thought leadership suffered a severe setback and many of the key individuals that adhered to the ANC narrative retreated into obscurity. Against the background of the choking climate of moral decay and the widening socio-economic inequality exacerbated by economic stagnation, conditions were potentially ripened for the emergence of a counter-discourse within the broader space of leftist politics. The conditions that triggered this possibility was, ironically, the Zuma-led ANC's culture of anti-intellectualism, which saw the ANC's national dominance in the realm of ideas decline and internal party diffidence set in and the ANC's intellectual leadership retreat.

Origins
The inevitable question however is why this radical and ideologically non-aligned student politics came about at the time when it did, given that the issues it raised were the social experience for the majority of South Africans since 1994. The key bread-and-butter

concerns of black students in tertiary education have revolved around financial and academic exclusions and the racist institutional ethos. Transformation at both the levels of form and content – the teaching staff, student admission policies, physical comforts of students such as accommodation and the actual body of knowledge and content – was at the centre of SASCO's agenda from the early 1990s.

Indeed, the period shortly after the 1994 democratic election saw an upsurge of radicalised student activism spurred on by financial and academic exclusions of largely poor black students and accusations of institutional racism (including at the staff level). Most of this student activism was visible at historically white universities such as Wits university, the University of Cape Town, the University of Natal, Rhodes University and so on. As bastions of white intellectual power, historically white universities reflected the racial power differential at multiple levels that rendered them vulnerable to the frustration of that segment of society that had been languishing in marginal socio-economic conditions. Historically black universities had challenges peculiar to them, mostly to do with access to finance. Most of these student struggles did not exclude violent forms of expression and it was at Wits that the first littering on campus happened as well as the most disruption of classes.

Most of these student struggles were led by SASCO and the demands were couched in ANC language. The issues that confronted tertiary education at the time reflected the wider struggles for socio-economic transformation led by the ANC government.

The comparison between the student-aligned resistance politics during the liberation struggle and the post-apartheid 'Fees Must Fall' student movement in South Africa throws up qualitative differences characteristic of the existential concerns of the two epochs.

Decoloniality of power: Biko, Fanon and intersectionality
Three texts helped to form the intellectual backbone of the Fees Must Fall movement. These are the writings of Steve Bantu Biko (*I write what I like*), Franz Fanon (*The Wretched of the Earth*) and works by Ngũgĩ wa Thiong'o, Mahmood Mamdani, Nelson Maldonado-Torres, amongst others, on decoloniality

Against the background of invisible bread-and-butter gains of the democratic breakthrough in April 1994, especially in education, decoloniality both as a political and epistemological movement has gained ascendancy in deconstructing post-political conditions and the ANC's liberation credentials in particular.

As an ideological platform of the Fees Must Fall movement, decoloniality is arguably much more expansive compared to the vision that characterised the philosophical platform of traditional liberation politics. For instance, ANC-driven politics pivots on key principles that define its DNA, such as unity, democracy, non-racialism and non-sexism. Traditional revolutionary politics, whether ANC, PAC or Azapo, drew their inspiration from known historical revolutionary traditions, including Marxism, African nationalism of the founding fathers such as Kwame Nkrumah, with Steve Biko and Franz Fanon probably being the only thinkers that straddled both worlds. For its side, and perhaps to its credit, the ANC had always acknowledged the multi-racial character of South Africa's demographic composition and therefore sought to embrace this given historical reality in its core principles while acknowledging the historical presence of 'race' as the organising principle of our political economy, a reality which in turn necessarily shapes its transformation agenda.

Inversely, along with other supplementary revolutionary currents such as Fanon and Biko, decoloniality of power has some historical depth in that it creates a coherent narrative that accounts for European colonial modernity that goes back to slavery and the matrices of power that have since 'othered' non-Europeans even as it puts Europeans at the existential apex. While decoloniality shares with all other liberation politics the starting points about freedom, racial justice and equality as well as the critique of racial capitalism, decoloniality goes further to question the nature of postcolonial relations. Its eclectic strands that reflect on the entire spectrum of power relations '… share an understanding that colonialism has not only displaced particular communities, but also their knowledges. It is to the recovery and re-articulation of those knowledges that these scholars and activists orient their academic work.'* It has also evinced some capacious view of human freedom by equally foregrounding all claims for freedom by the full spectrum of the subaltern, so that the struggle is not just limited to race and gender but embraces the lesbian, gay, bisexual and transgender (LGBT) community, what Sabelo Gatsheni-Ndlovu called 'contemporary human issues'. The

---

* https://globalsocialtheory.org/topics/decoloniality/

latter is captured by the rubric of intersectionality.

Yet, the Fees Must Fall movement tends to approach the notion of 'race' in a way that tends to essentialise its existence. For instance, its ideological articulations do not seem to move from the position that racial injustices must be addressed as a step towards a non-racial future but are coagulating within the category of 'race'. This seems to go against the grain of the Fanonian paradigm, which clearly seeks to go beyond 'race' as a colonial project in the quest for a new humanity. Conceding to the all-too-seductive trappings of racialist thinking may imperceptibly undo the lofty humanist gains of rebuilding human society in a fashion transcending the limitation of this sordid historical inheritance.

It would not be a stretch to submit that the decoloniality and kindred philosophical tenets advanced by the Fees Must Fall movement may be prefiguring a new political dawn in South African. Given its uncanny ability to make an explicit link between the student issues and the wider socio-economic landscape, signalling the fact that South Africa is on the cusp of new political possibilities whereby the business-as-usual agenda pursued by traditional revolutionary politics is coming to an end. Although elitist in that it is a student movement which is yet to unleash its full might of its political impact on wider society in both palpable and irreversible ways, the Fees Must Fall movement is a rapture that heralds a new era qualitatively different from anything that has come before it.

Lastly, the Fees Must Fall movement seems to be a worldwide phenomenon that both inspires and feeds off itself. It has foregone the stereotypical ways of revolutionary politics with organisation and leadership, and prefers a dispersed form of politics, infiltrating organs of civil society, thereby diffusing revolutionary ideas. This differs from SASCO in that SASCO saw itself as the nursery for the national political movement. This conceptual difference in approach shows that South African and indeed world politics will never be the same again!

Intellectual openings and policy closures: The many faces of higher education transformation

Busani Ngcaweni and Robert Nkuna

AT THE HEIGHT OF THE #RhodesMustFall and #FeesMustFall campaigns in 2015, very peculiar things happened at the level of public discourse. Amid heated arguments and contests for hegemony, new and old voices weighed in on debates, throwing volleys of reason and absurdities.

For example, respected author Allister Sparks made a statement suggesting that apartheid architect Hendrik Verwoerd was 'a smart man'. Sparks is routinely referred to as an intellectual and veteran journalist with more than half a century of speaking truth to power. As expected, Sparks's comments generated a flurry of attacks as it was widely believed that his statement was an insensitive tribute to a brute and bigot. He lost some credibility as a result but many commentators stood by him in an apparent assertion of his freedom of speech. Mcebo Dlamini, at the time a Wits law student and high profile 'Fallist', made a statement to the extent that he admired Adolf Hitler's 'charisma' and 'organisational skill'. Dlamini was equally criticised and disciplinary action taken by the university for putting Wits into disrepute. According to the Wits university vice chancellor, Professor Adam Habib, Dlamini's comments were 'racist and offensive in the extreme'.

If Sparks's comment was a mere value judgement, as some have opined, and not necessarily acclamation of Verwoerd, the question then arises: Do value judgements have values? In other words, can someone, without administering an IQ test, affirm another person as being smart, even if the balance of evidence overwhelmingly demonstrates that his supposed above-average IQ was morally bankrupt to the point of condemning a country to racial polarisation and socio-economic injustice?

Conscientious people are bound by normative standards or values to make judgements based on the totality of experience and effect. This means we should judge Lionel Messi by the extent to which he uses his talents to help his team win games and to advance football in general, not just by how well he can handle a football as an individual. Verwoerd's smartness as adjudicated by Sparks did not advance South Africa or any progressive human endeavour. He made South Africa the skunk of the world.

But this article is more about the authoritarian leadership of Habib than about the hypocrisy of Sparks, palpable coincidences notwithstanding. The fallout from Dlamini's 'I love Hitler' comments and his subsequent removal from the SRC presidency have added fuel to the raging transformation discourse in South Africa.

The Dlamini saga cannot be treated as an isolated case; it coincides with mass campaigns demanding qualitative transformation in higher education. At the epicentre of the storm are historically white universities – Cape Town (UCT), Wits, Rhodes, KwaZulu-Natal and Stellenbosch. These were citadels of white privilege under apartheid, and the charge from students and academics is that they remain so.

As student leaders in the mid-1990s, during the mass campaigns led by the South African Students' Congress demanding the transformation of higher education, we are compelled to take a look at the latest developments. What is happening represents the unfinished business of the struggle for transformation. This discussion should not be limited to the latest events but should deal with the entire ecosystem of higher education, from the discourse on academic freedom, curriculum design and student welfare to general governance issues.

Our contribution is not confined to the Dlamini saga, but it would be remiss not to comment on certain subtexts that have a long-term bearing on the governance of higher education. Two significant issues emerge from the press release issued by Habib announcing the removal of Dlamini from the SRC. The vice chancellor's unilateral decision to remove a sitting member of the SRC without canvassing the views of other SRC members, student organisations and the student community in general is tragic. Even if his right to remove an SRC president emanates from the SRC constitution or the rules of the university, we still argue that such a provision is out of sync with the gains of students' popular struggles to open the doors of learning and culture, and for meaningful participation in the governance of higher-education institutions.

Democratic student representative bodies were born on the terrain of struggle and thus are central to the discourse of transformation and academic freedom. The issue of academic freedom should not be limited to academics; students are full members of the academy and they too should enjoy the right to express themselves freely, as long as they do not violate the constitutional rights of others.

Habib would most definitely know this, given his role in the chaotic episodes at what was then the University of Durban-Westville in the 1990s. He could have led by example, allowing all stakeholders to express their views on an issue affecting them. When someone demonstrates poor comprehension of history, Habib should rehabilitate them using the best weapon in the university's arsenal: knowledge.

Now that he is removed, Dlamini will not learn history on the streets. Academic freedom (and freedom of expression in general) and student governance is not divisible; they reinforce each other.

Yes, there was a previous charge and conviction for alleged harassment against Dlamini, but that was not executed. That process, we are told, was exhausted. Just earlier this year, Dlamini was a national hero when he led a successful fundraising campaign to support poor students.

In Habib's words, Dlamini put Wits into disrepute. But which due process made that finding? Academics advocate due process when they challenge state authorities, so they cannot be excused from normative undertakings such as transparency, inclusivity and due process.

There is nothing illegal about Dlamini's views in the South African legal context, though it does show political naïvety for someone from the Congress tradition to align himself with a man who saw black people as sub-humans and killed at least two million of them, besides the millions of others he killed. Hitler, most definitely, was an evil man.

Still, Dlamini did not break any law and it is doubtful that Wits's own code of conduct outlaws such expressions. There have been several other instances at Wits where students and academics have openly expressed racist and prejudiced comments. They too will have to be expelled then, like the engineering lecturer who told his students that blacks fail engineering because they cannot think in 3D!

South Africans remain divided in the appraisal of our history. There is no consensus on who are the heroes to be celebrated by all South Africans. Paul Kruger, for example, is revered in the Afrikaner community but seen as a colonialist by black people, which explains the 'Kruger must fall' campaign to have his statute removed from the Pretoria city centre. It is also offensive to black people when some white Afrikaners wave the old apartheid flag that for many black people is no different from the Nazi swastika. Instead of getting bogged down with Hitler, we have to come to terms with our own Malans, Verwoerds and Bothas.

The university, as the foremost meeting place of learning for people from different backgrounds, should play a facilitative role instead of using a rule-book bound managerial language to manage difficult issues and stifle possible debates. UCT has done much better at this in recent times.

Understandably, since 1994 universities have become big businesses and therefore compete with each other to gain and maintain good reputations to attract sponsors and partners throughout the world. This is a good thing. But when it is overdone this 'look good' perspective may have unintended consequences as universities start to shy away from controversies and do everything possible to avoid negative publicity. But once a university takes such a posture, the nation is doomed. Universities are supposed to construct and deconstruct long-held beliefs and ideas in society. The university's general leaning towards postmodernism, which allows renewed social enquiry into traditional approaches to life and things around us, should enable discourse even on difficult and complicated issues. This should be done within and outside the classroom.

We argue that Habib's statement on Dlamini was a public-relations exercise for the university rather than dealing with simmering dynamics in the broader society, dynamics that unavoidably find space in the university.

Placing the university in the right frame of mind is key to the unfinished business of transforming higher education in South Africa. Other matters, such as the increase in the number of black academics and the need for a curriculum that supports national research, development and industrialisation needs, remain crucial.

As former student leaders, we argue that a university should be the last place from which students are expelled for their views. Universities should help students understand society, teach them responsibility and guide them in the journey towards self-discovery.

We, too, made grave mistakes and were forgiven by society. We were young and reckless. We went through political education. We learned.

The idea of exclusion remains archaic, undemocratic and uncharacteristic of the apex of human endeavour – the university – where we expect responsible intellectual discourse to bloom without using blunt bureaucratic instruments to censure dissent. We all know the impact of expulsions from higher education by apartheid administrators – young people lost the opportunity to learn and their futures were stunted. In the end, it is society that lost out.

This article was first written in May 2015.

The meaning and interpretation of the #FeesMustFall movement:* Draft thesis

David Maimela

TRYING TO MAKE SENSE OF political events retrospectively, through theorising, is not an easy exercise because often in our public discourse political events tend to pass with little interrogation due to the tyranny of the sound bite which has been made more pervasive by new media (aka social media). The #FeesMustFall movement had generated numerous analysis of it in the public. The missing link, however, is critical abstract analysis to accompany or even underwrite the political analysis. This chapter attempts a high-level interrogation of the issues presented by the #FeesMustFall movement in the form of some draft theses.

These draft theses were first written in October 2015 but they have since been updated, hopefully with greater lessons and insights from hindsight. This attempt at high-level theoretical interrogation straddles various levels of analysis: philosophical, historical, political, strategic and tactical.

Just little over two years since the students protested it is probably still too early to fully understand the meaning of these protests, let alone interpret them. Of concern to the author is whether the events that began in October 2015 in our higher education institutions will

---

* The author understands the #FeesMustFall movement to comprise other student protests in the country, namely, the #RhodesMustFall, #DecoloniseTheCurriculum, #FreeEducationInOurLifetime, as well as the often confused and confusing missed opportunity: #FeesHaveFallen.

deliver or rather aid a revolutionary change, as was the case in the past whenever the student movement rose. So the question arises: Is there a direct link between the student grievances, struggles and methods with broader societal struggles for social justice? Is the link a necessary one? And how do the students understand and represent it?

For instance, without drawing comparisons, the June 16 movement and struggles had linkages with the wider liberation movement and indeed the struggle for freedom. In a sense, and it has become common cause, the June 16 movement propelled the momentum towards victory against the apartheid regime. In comparison, the #FeesMustFall movement appears to have somewhat fizzled out and perhaps this has to do with matters of strategy and tactics. This does not mean that certain victories were not won. And certainly, it does not mean that the movement did not capture the hearts and minds of the people. Attempts at linking with wider struggles in society were made, namely, solidarity with workers on the outsourcing grievance. However, these were not sustained and neither were alliances.

Thesis 1: In philosophy, the protests confirm the relative superiority and correctness of the materialist worldview.

What comes first between thought (consciousness) and matter? Put otherwise, does consciousness have primacy over matter? This is an age-old philosophical question between protagonists such as Hegel and Marx over centuries. It is a debate which was later synthesised by Engels but the debate still rages on up to this day, essentially between idealists and materialists.

Hegel basically argued that consciousness has primacy over matter, that is, consciousness and human attitudes inform and shapes our material world. Marx argued the opposite. He posited that matter has primacy over consciousness, that is; the objective material world informs and shapes our consciousness and human attitudes. As a synthesis, Engels argued that whereas matter is foundational, ideas also exercise their influence about how we view reality and they temper with how we exercise our human agency.

It can be argued in relative terms that since the student protests initially had no prominent role for mainstream student political formations (which normally function as organs for organised political education and politicisation), the harsh material conditions of social exclusion conspired to shape the political consciousness of the students.

However, others may argue that political education takes various forms and can be found outside 'mainstream/organised' political formations and as a result, ideas of various sorts, from alternative sources, conspired to shape the manner in which the students understand their objective material reality and consequently what they need to do to change their circumstances for the better.

And yet, others can argue that the struggle for liberation, the student movement histories across generations and the historical global Free Education Campaign has exercised influence on the memory and consciousness of the current generation to act out the heroic deeds they did. In the process, it is possible that some of the protesters will be politicised and as a result, consider political activism and political affiliation on a permanent basis. No doubt, some of our future leaders will emerge from the ranks of this generation. In other words, the rise of this movement is, in general, a positive development.

Thesis 2: Understanding the meaning of the protests in relation to society: The ideas generated throughout the protest, starting with #RhodesMustFall, have certainly shaped a new reality at various spheres of society beyond the campus, although with missed opportunities.

In this instance, the ideas, both new and revisited ones, are exercising their influence on how various actors from government to political parties, university managers and other interests act towards the polity, the student movement and the political economy of education.

Based on the pressure and ideas emerging out of the protest movement, the expectation is that it will not be 'business as usual' in many spheres of society, that is, if the full meaning of the protest is properly captured by those in positions of power. Those in positions of power refer to individuals and organisations. These can be in the form of a singular pole of power or a coalition of governance, either within the state or the broader polity. The assumption is that power, although highly concentrated in the state, is equally dispersed across society.

Given the argument that the movement has thawed in recent months, the ideas generated in the protests may disappear and hopefully be recaptured later in our historical development process.

Without listing the various contending ideas, it can be said that the ideas have one objective: an attempt to define how to achieve total emancipation which will necessarily lead to a better quality of life.

Among others, two of the realities that these various ideas have spawned is the re-awakening of a certain brand of Black Consciousness and a new sense of black intellectual solidarity. For instance, at university level, there is now a common understanding that institutional culture and curriculum stagnation must be challenged, in both black or white universities.

Thesis 3: The meaning of the protests in themselves and sectorally are profound, epochal and generational.
The rise of the movement is also the result of the sheer demographic changes in our society. And higher education is undoubtedly affected by these changes. In the forefront of the protests are youth who were mostly born after 1994. Their protest is an emphatic statement of disapproval of the lack of transformation in the sector. The students are asking the simple and yet profound questions: what is the meaning of struggle and freedom? What is the pace and the quality of change in the university when juxtaposed with the expectations and promise of 1994? What is the direction of this change, if any? Who benefits?

It seems that the students are saying, by and large, that they are merely marking time. Managers of universities have failed the transformation project and so has the government and other poles of power in society. The fact that a generation later, we return to the questions* raised by Mamdani and Makgoba means that we have indeed been marking time. Why else return to the same questions more than a decade later? And certainly, if we do not respond to the questions of the students decisively, a generation later, we will ask the same questions again and thus continue the foolishness of marking time.

Thesis 4: The fundamental sources of the evolving political conflict are to be found in broader society and the political economy.
If students are members of the community first before they are

---

* These questions refer to the controversial manner in which both professors and scholars were isolated and excluded from universities of Cape Town and Wits respectively in the 90s, thus leading to the sharpening of contestation about transformation in general and curriculum change in particular.

students, then it follows that the underprivileged social status of the poor and working-class students confronts the prospects and indeed realities of either continuity or discontinuity in the struggle for change and social mobility, both in the university setting and in society more broadly.

Being at university represents upward mobility in the social ladder. This is a privilege reserved for a few in an unequal society given the high costs associated with sending and keeping a child at university. Unfortunately, this privilege soon turns into pain when the very same students face the vagaries of backward and untransformed universities, an experience cited by many students to be alienating and depressing. For others they soon ride the privilege train and become indifferent to the students who come from poor backgrounds.

Financial exclusion has bigger implications for society. For instance, those who drop out due to financial reasons return back to hopelessness in the community and their burden of social exclusion is equally difficult and painful to bear. This is the case because the economy has limited options for those without skills or education. And the burden on public goods increases.

For the privileged students, the continuity and expansion of privilege is the likelihood, but as the state fails at achieving inclusive economic development, various factors emerge to expose the vulnerabilities and insecurities of the privileged student too.

Just like the state, the university establishes its legitimacy through public accountability and being inclusive and if it fails as it does now, then the insecurities and vulnerabilities of all associated with the university rises.

In some of the campuses, academics exposed the illegitimacy of the university and the state when they joined the protest and formed human shields against the police and campus security and engaged in further mass protests. The students and academics have a common material interest: the sustenance of the university. The academic must eke out a living and pursue knowledge; the student must learn and graduate. At times, it can be said that their interests are co-dependent. The possibility of a cross-cultural, class and racial solidarity arises out of this context.

It is also true that some white people have consciously committed class or even racial suicide for a variety of reasons. Some sections of the privileged classes and strata may feel ethically compelled to support causes of this nature and that is a function of consciousness, as well as survival and the search for legitimacy.

Others may argue that as changes happen in the economy, the social position and interests of both black and white middle-class families will tend to converge and thus there is a possibility that the two groups are beginning to face similar pressures in terms of income and expenditure, albeit at different levels of intensity.

In an unequal society and untransformed universities skewed power relations can either be reproduced or broken down depending on the variable power and position of the protagonists. Although the dominant power structures have been consistently challenged for the past 21 years, they seem to have reached some turning point in the last five years or so. In other words, it can be said that contradictions are sharpening and power is tilting in favour of progressive forces of change in the higher education sector. The forces of reaction have basically dug their own grave due to their failure to reform the sector.

The expectation is that education (including further and higher education) is a right not a privilege, and a public good that the government should provide for all who wish to access it. In addition, this situation is compounded by the ideological struggles and legitimacy crisis of the dominant ideas in society, which is why, in search of a material and cultural revolution, the students are asking: why is the university and the curriculum content not decolonised? What are the values that underpin education provision? What is the meaning of struggle and freedom? Why has the academy not decolonised and freed itself from coloniality? Is our cultural state of affairs commensurate with our aspirations for material advancement?

However, one wonders whether the same questions about the university were sufficiently asked about society as a whole, whether the movement paid sufficient attention to questions of tactics in the execution of struggle, particularly the building and strengthening of alliances. Can the university and the struggle to change it play a role in transforming society and, in turn, how can it learn from society?

The latter set of questions are important for the interrogation of the seeming failure of the movement to link these organic struggles between community and university. Was the movement itself trapped in elitism and pretending to be progressive and radical?

Thesis 5: Throughout history, students' struggles have often inspired society beyond campus perimeters.

The African students movement during the struggle against official colonialism organised against 'deculturation and depersonalisation' of the African. So, even youth formations, outside the youth wings of liberation movements, recognised the centrality of national liberation struggles and the importance of restoring the human dignity of Africans. Recently, the Occupy Wall Street movement was, in part, a conglomeration of student protest against the rising national student debt in the United States and elsewhere in the world.

In South Africa, when the liberation movements were banned, the flame for freedom inside the country was kept alight by organisations such as the South Africa Students' Organisation (SASO), the Soweto SRC before, during and after 1976. The Black Consciousness Movement (BCM) itself was inspired by the student movement and so are many community service projects by the youth. Before he was killed by the brutal apartheid regime, Onkgopotse Tiro taught in Soweto and did political education and organising work in the build up to June 1976. Today, the campus struggles also inspire the youth and workers, on and off campus.

Once more these examples illustrate the point about the consistent linkages between student and community struggles. Did the #FeesMustFall movement understand this history out of necessity?

Thesis 6: Revolutions are always led by the youth.

Throughout history, the youth have often occupied the forward trenches in revolutions and struggles of all sorts. A recent example is the so-called Arab Spring in North Africa and the Middle East. We know about the roaring 1980s of the Young Lions in South Africa. The people who flooded the liberation army camps during apartheid were mainly youth. We also know that Steve Biko died at the young age of 33. Che Guevara and Fidel Castro were in their 20s when they fought for revolution, and so was Nelson Mandela and Thabo Mbeki, who was the youngest person ever to address the United Nations (UN) Special Committee Against Apartheid at the age of 22 in 1964. Today, vice chancellors, who were all once contemporaries of the above-mentioned young revolutionaries, consider student leaders immature, clueless and irresponsible. Indeed, they believe there should not be a meaningful engagement with students.

Because the burdens of the past weigh heavily on the shoulders of the present generation, a meaningful intergenerational dialogue is necessary as a common space of learning, always.

Thesis 7: The issues are not necessarily new but have been recast and presented by new faces and voices.
The current struggle for transformation in higher education, of which funding and fees is the main element, is not new. What we see is a continuation of earlier struggles, if you consider the whole experience of the colony. The most assuring part about the current generation is the fact that more than half the time they do not de-historicise the struggle, they actually build on their predecessors. Apparently, the Stellenbosch students are saying: 'We have actually not yet begun our own struggles, we are just finishing off what our parents started.'

In other words, the students have a great sense of history and are 'politically educated' in the broadest sense of the phrase. They are effectively dispelling the myth of 'born frees' in South Africa. History does not proceed in a linear fashion as if there is a Chinese wall between the past, present and future. In truth, the present is born of the past and the future is born of the two and together they form one continuum.

So what makes the current struggles since 2015 so pronounced? It is possible that two factors came into play to make their voices appear louder. In the first instance, we must commend their efforts to use the latest technology to make these struggles louder and reach many audiences faster. Social media has made it possible to make the issues into a national dialogue. The second instance is the reality that we have a new generation since 1994, a generation that is engaged in an important national dialogue about the meaning of struggle and freedom. In the townships, at the forefront of local protests are young people in their large numbers. At the universities, particularly in historically white institutions, many black young people are engaged in similar struggles about social inclusion and exclusion.

Other notable endeavours can be seen in the performing arts and music fields where this new generation is engaged in this profound search for the meaning of struggle and freedom.

Thesis 8: For 21 years, the system has been characterised by 'stagnation and tension'.
At a policy level, questions regarding better access and transformation have not been sufficiently addressed. But the university environment is faced with many pressures: managing and influencing diversity, addressing social change, sustaining the higher education system and the environment while helping to transform society more broadly. In other words, how does the university improve and maintain teaching, research and learning infrastructure, how does the university become energy efficient, how does it contain costs, etc.

Another way to illustrate the tension and even contradictions is to paraphrase one academic at the Second Higher Education Transformation Summit in October 2015 in Durban who asked the question: Is the university not curtailing academic freedom if it allows for the violent crushing of democratic protest by students, criminalising protest and victimising student leaders? Is the presence of police on campus not intimidation to academia and threatening to academic freedom? And we should know that if we fail to address the core problems of the system, they will keep escalating and the academy will be under immense pressure on many fronts.

There is a general sense that higher education transformation has stagnated and as a result, tensions abound. It is through the agency of all progressive partners in the sector that the next potential and frontier of progress in the sector may come. Otherwise, the sector risks losing legitimacy and thus failing to contribute to human progress.

Thesis 9: The system is governed by the twin rules of institutional autonomy and public accountability. Institutional autonomy is well established and has flourished, whereas public accountability is not and has neither been achieved nor served.
The universities have used institutional autonomy and academic freedom to undermine public accountability. To date, most of the goals in 'White Paper 3 on Higher Education' and many ministerial investigative report recommendations have not been realised. This has undermined the power and legitimacy of the state as key driver of transformation in the sector.

For example, failure to have meaningful community engagement by some institutions means that public accountability is undermined and so is failure to produce black and female academics, researchers and professors. Lack of diversity at the level of producing these professionals means that diversity is not seen as a powerful tool to enrich our cultural experience (history, knowledge production, critical discourse, teaching, etc.). All cultures are enhanced by interaction with other cultures. The failure of diversity at this level undermines our ability to contribute to human civilisation.

Others can also argue that autonomy is not ideologically neutral anyway. Whose autonomy is it? Who benefits? For instance, if the university retain their autonomy to set fees, set admission requirements, force students to buy academic records, deny them access to graduation ceremonies when owing fees, impose re-registration fees, force student to buy their first student cards, call students 'clients', etc. Whose autonomy is it when things like these happen?

Thesis 10: The protests are a continuation of the internationalist struggle for free education.
This thesis really points to the values of human solidarity and the interconnectedness of humanity. History records that, even outside the International Union of Students (IUS) and All Africa Students Union (AASU), for many decades students have waged relentless struggles across the world in pursuit of free education. In 2012, students across the United States protested in many major cities as part of the Occupy movement but also to mark the moment when the national student debt reached 1 trillion US dollars. They protested demanding 'debt-free degrees'.

Here in South Africa, the student movement across political and ideological divisions has stood for free quality public education. It is important to note that free education is not necessarily a socialist ideal or demand, with many successful models found in both socialist and capitalist countries. Here in South Africa, many ideas have been proposed and ignored on how best to achieve free education. The Freedom Charter of 1955 upholds the ideal of free education.

It makes no logical sense to speak of the National Health Insurance and not the equivalent: a National Fund for Free Education. South Africa has no choice but to succeed in providing social protection, health and education for all. But, probably the lasting solution may come from technology, bar the rise of monopoly industries or firms that may scramble for commercialisation. The traditional university as we know it today is fading!

The announcement of 'free higher education for the poor and working class' in December 2017 is a historic victory in a historical global struggle for access to education. The next frontier of this struggle is around sustenance of the policy, as well as the fight against student debt. The victory is only partial. The struggle continues.

Thesis 11: The protests are questioning whether universities are truly democratic spaces. Clearly, they are not.
The commitment to democratisation means that we should strive to democratise all our public spaces and institutions, especially so that they gain more legitimacy and become more inclusive. For some time now, the higher education sector has been grappling with how best to govern and the results show a mixed picture. For some institutions, a well-run university is one that conforms to formalities: compliance with the so-called 'good governance' principles, a phrase which simply refers to corporate culture and capture. This means that:

- Many of our councils see themselves as corporate boards running corporate entities and our vice chancellors see themselves as CEOs.
- By and large, the end game is about keeping a positive balance sheet to the detriment of all other important values, activities and outcomes.
- Increasingly, almost all universities have adopted the corporate language and culture of 'client-service provider' relations. Our students are now clients and so the fundamental relationship of learning and teaching is through money. Those who have money have easy access. Those without money find it hard to gain access.

In conclusion, a university that embraces attributes of the corporate sector cannot be said to be a democratic space nor can it fully be built or operate on the basis of democratic culture. In a corporate space and culture, cash is king and if cash is king, then before you speak or participate, you must pay. That kind of culture tends to affirm authority and power over negotiation and democratic engagement. Authority often compels compliance, whereas democratic engagement often listens, questions and is inclusive.

Even structurally and process-wise, universities are not necessarily the best of democratic spaces. Councils are not democratic in form and content. The principles of representation, fairness, freedom, equality, justice and accountability are not reflected in our councils. The process to appoint vice chancellors is not truly democratic. We need councils or governance structures that are as democratic as SRCs at the very least. Vice chancellors can be elected in a college-like system, instead of being appointed. Universities can be governed by differently constituted general assemblies, based on the principles outlined herein.

It is clear that the movement has produced more questions than answers. Yes, because change is the only constant, progress produces new conditions out of which new contradictions are born. The movement and the struggles it spawned were not in vain. As some of the draft theses suggest, a number of victories have been scored, some setbacks have been encountered and some missed opportunities have occurred.

Some of the critical success factors for any movement are leadership and organisation. It is not sufficient to simply hold an idea, upon which you wage struggles and protest. The idea must be anchored coherently on organisation and leadership. The three can take various forms depending on time and space.

However, the movement bordered on anarchy when most of the activists insisted that there is no hierarchy or central decision-making, even though many could see a central core of leaders. As a result, two of the major weaknesses and momentums lost, hopefully not forever, are the building of alliances, as well as a stronger articulation of the organic link between students and the community.

Otherwise, there are many lessons learned and many victories to be celebrated!

Forgive us Biko for we have betrayed you
Gugu Ndima

I WATCHED A MAN in his 60s battle with a choice of retaining his pride or surrendering it in the hope that he can survive poverty. At first sight, he looked like a resident employee of that institution of higher learning, as he made his way into the food court. Maybe he was an employee. Dressed in a suit, carrying a newspaper and a black folder under one arm and a plastic shopping bag in the other, he gracefully but cautiously walked in. As he came close to one of the food counters, he slowed down, his eyes slowly scanning to see if anyone was looking at him. Students were minding their business and it was still morning. What he did thereafter seemed like something he did habitually. He walked to a nearby trash can and looked once again to see if any eyes were on him.

He tucked the newspaper tighter under his arm and moved closer to the bin, then took out a box, opened it quickly and fortunately found leftovers. A glaring mien of relief came over his face as he was saved the humiliation of digging deeper into the trash can. He quickly went to one of the food counters with the box and squeezed out tomato sauce placed on a side table for patrons. In that busy food court that day, no one noticed him.

He placed the shopping bag on the floor, taking a seat on one of the many tables available for customers, unfolded his newspaper on the table, pretending to be bothered with the headlines. He hurriedly took out two slices of brown bread from the packet, dabbed them in the tomato sauce and chowed them down. The rapidness in which he ate his meal wasn't a reflection of pleasure or indulgence but submission to a famished stomach, a desperate need to avert hunger. Had he allowed his pride to win, he would have further shrunk into starvation.

I managed to get a closer look from a safe distance without giving away that I had been watching him. His shoes carried a dusty tale of a long journey to where he managed to rest. The uneven soles of his shoes betrayed the secrets he was trying to conceal about his poverty and strain. His clothes spoke volumes about a man who once had hopes of walking into a dignified place he could call a workplace. His tired face, vaguely concealing his pain, fatigue and rage, was well camouflaged by his elegant mannerism, demonstrating that his actions weren't that of a mad man, just a man adversely betrayed by a democratic system which once carried hope that after 1994 he and many others like him would witness the restoration of the pride and dignity of black men.

Greetings Father of Black Consciousness, greetings Tata. I greet you from the future, the land of democracy, a rainbow nation as we are now called. A future free from legislated apartheid, yet still chained by unlegislated tentacles of the draconian system.

For some odd reason I have been battling to write this piece until I bore witness to this moment. I bear witness daily to men and women eating from garbage cans, some others who collect trash to buy food. Poverty has been normalised in the democratic dispensation, yet as apartheid systemically excluded and affected the black majority, poverty still has the face of an African. Dilapidated buildings in hazardous conditions in urban areas are homes to communities of our people who resemble the living dead. Black men and women are carcasses of radicalised capitalism and appendages of its production system. The best description for this economic catastrophe is what Frantz Fanon captured as 'The wretched of the earth'.

It would be injustice and bordering on deception if I just painted one side of the democratic picture. South Africa as a country has gone through various transitions – some cosmetic, others tangible. I don't carry a dom pass. My movements are no longer restrained or dictated by a political system. Black people have opportunities which were historically preserved for a certain race. Democracy gave rise to a new era and a new nation born from the constitution. The constitution as envisaged by your generation is an embodiment of the

Freedom Charter legislating a social contract for all South Africans, recognising rights and equality for everyone. This is one supreme document which has been portrayed as the panacea for all forms of justice. Yet ideal as it seems, constitutionalism has been the greatest protector of economic injustices experienced by Africans and it is the perpetuator of white privilege. The constitution has a plethora of rights i.e. rights to education, health, basic services, life, freedom of expression etc. Yet the central component of realising all those rights, which is land and property, is still in the hands of architects of colonialism and apartheid. These are the tentacles of apartheid hollowing out the notion of freedom in its entirety for Africans.

While one respects and understands the role of democracy in advancing the struggle, it couldn't possibly have been the end in itself, as democracy can't seem to find expression in the economy. There are more changes in conceptual narratives of the struggle than actual actions taken to advance it. We have moved into a trend of subdividing freedom into 'freedoms', giving it various phases of transitions. One can't argue that even revolutions have stages as Marx and Engels stated in *The Communist Manifesto* (1848), yet it seems that the concepts in the democratic dispensation are moving the goal post, which was the essence of why liberation movements and organisations were born in the first place. People joined the struggle because they were born into it; they experienced and lived it. They required no theoretical explanation as struggle was life. However, even my generation is being born into the struggle; it might not seem as violent as your generation's yet it remains the same trajectory with the same ultimate goal. I do not believe that there are good and bad struggles because all struggles affect the livelihood of a human. People might not be experiencing the whip of a policeman on their backs but there's a cracking whip of capitalism that lashes on workers and the poor daily.

I have the utmost respect for heroes and heroines of your generation and those that came before you. Your fearlessness and gallantry became the cement towards liberation. However, I will admit that your generation in this new democratic dispensation is fast becoming a curse to us – the destroyers of our future and replicates of oppressors. There is a growing sense of entitlement amongst leaders who led during the struggle, that for some reason we owe them for realising their goal in the struggle. What then of the whole notion of voluntarism in the struggle and the realisation that participation in the struggle was a collective effort for all people and even for generations to come?

This sense of entitlement has made leaders more comfortable with the enemy. We are fast being robbed of a chance to fight for the realisation of our generational mission and for future generations to come. One would hope that those who were in the frontlines in the battlefields with the enemy would have a greater sense of urgency in securing a future which they struggled for and of which we are still struggling for. Betrayal has become a glaring phenomenon in the democratic dispensation where Africans are becoming poorer and those Africans that have escaped these realities are hegemonising their narrow interests with neo-colonialists.

The apparatus of oppression is no longer just characterised by race; class interests are becoming more and more prevalent yet the irony is that the race of the poor and marginalised is still as black as it was during your years. People are being fed the constitution all in the name of reconciliation. We have elevated reconciliation and nation building over seeking socio-economic justice.

No white man has paid for apartheid atrocities; no white company has been ceded over to Africans. Yet our constitution speaks of equality. The value chain in corporate South Africa is still lily white, where the same corporates that made profit during apartheid are just as wealthy and ownership patterns haven't changed. The worst aspect of this reality is that even new players in the economy are still white and the system of this democracy has allowed perverse monopolies to thrive.

The infrastructure developed in our communities has only opened gateways for more white corporations to further exploit our people as workers and take their money as consumers. A lot of reforms have been undertaken but blacks are still relegated to the second economy. The political and bureaucratic elite have embraced foreign investors over stimulating domestic development. Our economy has been outsourced to more foreigners under the guise of alternative investment. Yet this image is one of voluntary neo-colonialism. Africans own nothing; this country's wealth is determined by currency rates in London, New York and Hong Kong. It seems we are led by a generation of leaders that can't imagine freedom without an oppressor, without his input on what freedom should be for the oppressed. There are rich black men in close proximity to the political elite yet their wealth makes no difference in the current status quo. Our liberation objectives are replaced by bureaucratic blueprints such as the National Development Plan, thus confining the majority of our people to survivalist modes of employment and businesses. It's become survival of the fittest as we embrace individual rights, in isolation of the collective.

I can't sit on the sidelines and blame your generation which has been leading since the dawn of democracy, for as part of my generation, I must take full responsibility for this betrayal too – the betrayal of the man I mentioned above, the betrayal of our people still living in the townships, the betrayal of all our forebears, as it seems we have become more content with imported notions of forgiveness and building a nation. How could we have forgiven those who never asked for forgiveness? It would be naïve of me to assume that it could have been that simple. So, for now I can only ask for forgiveness and draw strength from your unrelenting spirit to fight beyond this protracted phase.

Forgive me, forgive us Biko for abdicating our responsibility to serve and trade our souls to become pimps prostituting our soil, wealth and children to neo-colonialists.

Forgive me, forgive us Biko for we know not that we are now a mere shadow of the very same oppressor that robbed us of you when the African child needed you to fight.

Forgive me, forgive us Biko for we might have even forgotten what it is to be black. Maybe we detest it to a point that we have conceded to the conceptions of white people on what is blackness.

Forgive me, forgive us Biko for the betrayal of the struggle of the African people, allowing greed and short sightedness to blind us to the promises of the white man.

Forgive me and forgive us for the man who leaves home in a suit only to scavenge in trash bins to keep poverty at bay. What has become of his rights to human dignity and right to life if he has no means to even realise those rights?

I might sound helpless, defeated and needy but my current realities don't make my struggle a choice but a necessity. My realities necessitate that I move on, fight on and that in the midst of all this despair, find courage to see beyond the pessimism. Giving up on my people is betraying myself, my forebears and your legacy. It is in the

hour of bleakness that a man's will is tested.
   Power to the people!

The ticking time bomb of youth unemployment

Qhama Bona

WHEN SOUTH AFRICA ATTAINED democracy in 1994, many heralded that achievement as a catalyst for the country to address its dark history of colonialism and apartheid. There can be no doubt that colonialism and apartheid have robbed black South Africans of the life they should have had. These unjust laws curtailed the potential of many black people. It also ensured that black people were landless in the country of their birth. Therefore, the 1994 democratic breakthrough was meant to reverse the legacy of colonialism and apartheid. Accordingly, the new democratic government of the African National Congress (ANC) put legislations in place that would help uplift the lives of black people. It also helped that the country adopted a new constitution and bill of rights that enshrined the rights of every South African.

The country's constitution is lauded by many as one of the best in the world. However, some share the belief that the constitution is another tool to protect white privilege by ensuring that their land does not get expropriated without compensation. But, even though the ANC government did a lot to ensure that the procedural side of democracy is fulfilled, it is the substantive side that leaves a lot to be desired. There is the belief that 24 years after the ANC government assumed power the lives of black people have not improved substantially. Admittedly, the ANC government will rattle many statistics about how its government has managed to provide houses, sanitation, electricity and other basic services to the people of South Africa. No one can disagree with that, but one can also point out that many people have not received some of the services that other communities have received. That is why the country is always faced with violent service delivery protests. People are angry because the ANC government has failed to transform the lives of all the people.

Today South Africa is rated as the most unequal society in the world according to its Gini coefficient. The country is faced with the quadruple challenges of grinding poverty, a stubborn unemployment rate, rocket-high inequality and repugnant corruption. But, it has been the scourge of unemployment in particular amongst black young people that has caused serious damage and led to other socio-economic ills that continue to halt the growth of a nation that showed great promise when it attained its freedom in 1994. As a result of the aforementioned social factors, many young people feel that the 1994 democratic breakthrough was not the ideal settlement for black people. Many of these young people are angry at the government as well as white monopoly capital that still controls most of the country's economy. This anger has surfaced in various ways, but it was at the 2015 Rhodes Must Fall (RMF) and Fees Must Fall (FMF) protests that the country felt the wrath of its angry young people. Both protests were motivated by the fact that the status quo, even inside the university, has not really changed. Indeed, education is still an extremely expensive commodity that only few can afford. That has resulted in the reproduction of apartheid patterns which ensure that many black people will be relegated to a life of hopelessness and obscurity.

However, the youth of today ensured that they will not accept this unfair reality. One is reminded of how Frantz Fanon in *The Wretched of the Earth* spoke of how each generation must discover its mission, fulfil it or betray it, in relative opacity It is clear that the youth of today are inspired by the words of people like Fanon. They draw on the fearlessness of luminaries such as Robert Sobukwe, Solomon Mahlangu, Steve Biko and Frantz Fanon to name a few. One would hear songs about these fearless revolutionaries being sung by students during the protests. But, most importantly, the youth have to fight the scourge of youth unemployment as well as to decolonise the universities that impose their colonial methods of doing things, which is reflected in their curriculums.

But, in order for one to understand the conundrum of youth unemployment it is imperative to look at the structure of the South African economy. In the 20th century this economy was mainly reliant on the mining sector which used the cheap labour from black people to enrich itself. That is why during that period mining was a pivotal industry in the South African economy. It is important even today, but it has definitely dwindled in terms of significance due to a variety of factors including the major drop in commodity prices. When the ANC government took charge in 1994, they tried to address this issue of the country's economy being mainly in the hands of white males. That is why Broad-Based Black Economic Empowerment (B-BBEE) was introduced and was portrayed as the panacea to resolving the country's economic woes. However, it turned out that B-BBEE was a policy designed to enrich politically connected individuals in the ANC. The biggest beneficiaries of B-BBEE are said to be Cyril Ramaphosa, Tokyo Sexwale, Patrice Motsepe, Mathews Phosa, Baleka Mbete, Saki Macozoma, Mzi Khumalo and Robert Gumede amongst many other ANC leaders. The common thread between all the aforementioned people is that they are politically connected individuals who amassed a great deal of wealth while not really working hard for it. B-BBEE makes it compulsory for companies to sell 26% of their stake to black consortiums. But then the government helps to finance these black oligarchs. So what you get is a small clique of inordinately rich black people who happen to have political connections, yet the overwhelming majority still live in squalor.

It is indictments against these people that unemployment and its related factors have been exacerbated whilst this comprador bourgeoisie have managed to get rich very quickly. Together with white monopoly capital, this black bourgeoisie has forgotten about the impoverished black majority. That is why the ANC government has employed policies that allow for the outsourcing of labour which means labour brokers benefit at the expense of people employed by them. That is why the students fought for the abolishment of outsourcing at universities. Outsourcing, as students argued, is a form of modern slavery as it is exploitative of workers and makes it easy to dispense with them when the employer does not see their need anymore. The students, however, are not going to tolerate outsourcing at their universities because it demeans as much as it exploits their black parents. It is this type of attitude that the youth of today ought to adopt, because their democratic government is no longer keen to tackle these issues or else they would have scrapped labour brokers a long time ago. At the 2007 Polokwane conference, the ANC had passed a resolution that labour brokers should be outlawed. Yet they have failed to implement their own resolution.

Whatever the successes of the ANC government are, statistics show that the ruling party has failed the black youth of South Africa. Admittedly, the issue of unemployment has a deep historical context and that can never be ignored. However, the ANC government should have done a lot more to uplift young black people as well as to up-skill them in order for them to enter the job market.

What you get are policies that do not really tackle the issue of youth unemployment decisively. Government will point to the fact that it introduced a youth wage subsidy. That subsidy is meant to encourage companies to employ young people by giving them incentives. But the argument against this policy is that it does not deal decisively with this issue as it merely scratches the surface. There has to be a radical policy shift from the ruling party in order to deal decisively with the issue of unemployment. But it is increasingly futile putting any trust into this ANC government.

The party is more preoccupied with protecting its corrupt leader, Jacob Zuma, rather than changing the lives of young people. There can be no arguments about the fact that Zuma is presiding over a kleptocratic state that is seemingly incapable of changing the lives of black people.

Seeing that the ANC government has abandoned its historic mission of liberating the black majority from economic bondage, it is important that the youth of today take responsibility for its future. Many young people have demonstrated that they have the capacity to create jobs for themselves. A culture of entrepreneurship amongst young people should be encouraged by all means. That will help them create new wealth and also be able to create jobs for other young people. But again it is extremely difficult for young people to start their own businesses if they do not receive the financial support they require. It is a well-known fact that banks are not keen to give out loans to people who do not have assets. That means young people cannot garner the capital needed to start their businesses. On the other hand, government is enriching 'tenderpreneurs' that are politically connected. It is also another well-known fact that tenders are merely used as a meal ticket for ANC cadres. It is precisely for this reason that the ANC cannot be depended upon in order to drive the agenda to radically transform South Africa's mainly white economy.

As a result of this ballooning youth unemployment, there is a great danger that South Africa could experience an Arab Spring of its own. When a large number of black youth are unemployed and loitering on the streets that is a perfect recipe for social upheaval. It is even more infuriating for these young people to see their white counterparts as well as a small minority of black people enjoying the fruits of this democracy. Yet, most of these young people are relegated to a life of poverty. One of these days, this growing army of unemployed black youth will rise and rebel against the status quo. When such an uprising happens, there is no telling about what they will do.

Therefore, it is imperative that this issue of unemployment together with the issue of land and that of the economy gets tackled expeditiously. It is in the best interests of all peace-loving South Africans to contribute to fighting this scourge of unemployment. The government, as well, has to change the way it is doing things. Clearly it cannot be business as usual when most young people are in such a dire situation. Already the crime rate in South Africa is excessively high and most of the perpetrators are young black people. They do not have many other alternatives because they were denied their right to education.

To conclude, it is clear to see that the issue of youth unemployment has become the biggest crisis facing this country. All the relevant stakeholders have not really tried to tackle this issue in a meaningful way. As a result of that, unemployment has become the single biggest socio-economic ill that derails South Africa's progress. But this generation of young people has to confront all these obstacles. It cannot afford to be derailed in its mission to build a South Africa that will truly restore the dignity of the black majority who are made to feel like unwelcome guests in the land of their birth. While white people together with a small elite of mostly ANC politically connected individuals continue to plunder the natural resources of this country whilst the overwhelming majority are forced to feed off the crumbs. The youth of today ought to fulfil their generational mission which RMF and FMF sparked or else history will not judge them kindly.

Decolonising where it matters most: TVET colleges

Wandile Ngcaweni

ACCESS TO EDUCATION IS a right most dear to black people in post-apartheid South Africa. Black people have emerged battered from a devastating history of colonial education, most importantly apartheid's Bantu Education policy made official by the passing of the Bantu Education Act of 1953. The Act disempowered black people by reducing their ability to fully participate in the labour market. It did so by undermining their ability to gain vocational, technical and tertiary education, thus reducing them to unskilled manual labourers.

The minister of native affairs at the time, Hendrik Verwoerd, is quoted as asking, 'What is the use of teaching the Bantu child mathematics when it cannot use it in practice?' (Qubeka, 2017). The white minority, on the other hand, received exceptional education and training, and acquired the requisite skills to compete in a job market that was confined to them.

It is understandable why many black people in South Africa are so passionate about their right to education and why they see universities as a symbol of the precious education that was denied them for so long.

There has been very little rigorous discussion in other higher education institutions other than universities, and the decolonisation debate has not reached Technical and Vocational Education and Training (TVET) colleges. These are often mislabelled in popular discourse as 'alternative' institutions when in fact they should be recognised as critical public universities in addressing the skills needed by a developing economy.

Context
In the *2016 Economic Outlook* report by the OECD, there were alarming findings about labour market trends in South Africa. The study revealed a growth in the numbers of young people who are neither employed nor in education or training – so-called 'NEETs'. These youths are most in danger of permanently being left out of the labour market. A Department of Higher Education and Training (2013: 3) analysis suggests that there were 3.2 million youth (aged 15–24) who were not in education, employment or training in 2011 while the Statistics South Africa 2017 Quarterly Labour Force Survey shows that 32.4% of youth aged 15–24 remained NEETs (2017: 11). In fact, it is so serious that more than one in five young people between the ages of 15 and 29 were low-skilled NEETs according to the 2016 OECD.

These statistics paint a bleak picture of the challenge of access to education at all levels in South Africa and particularly in higher education. They suggest limited success in expanding access to education in South Africa, and particularly to higher education. Furthermore, there is a challenge of skills mismatch in South Africa that remains unattended to.

The South African government has acknowledged that TVET colleges are central to skilling South African youth and the unemployed. The National Development Plan (NDP) highlights the intention to fundamentally support and expand the skills employment sector in the battling South African job economy and effectively lift many young South Africans out of absolute poverty.

Historical context
There has been, since the 19th and 20th centuries, a contested opinion on which form of education is more important/relevant. For instance, in the United States, two leaders emerged opposing each other. Booker T. Washington drew from the philosophy of education for self-help (technical), while W.E.B. Du Bois was an advocate for college education in the liberal arts (university). In South Africa, Dr John Langalibalele Dube opened, in line with the philosophy of

Booker T. Washington, a school for skills and self-help: the Ohlange Institute. The school was meant to impart technical training to young black people, of which the architects of apartheid would seek to disprove for decades by denying black people opportunities for quality vocational and technical training.

H.F. Verwoerd thought of black people as 'hewers of wood and drawers of water', meaning that black people were only good for physical labour not cognitive employment, going as far as making policy of his beliefs in the form of the Bantu Education Act of 1953. If this was the condition in which our parents grew up, who can blame them for wanting their kids to attend university? TVETs, apart from their quality concerns, might be seen to be in line with Verwoerd sentiments by our parents who experienced Bantu education.

The German case study
We could look to Germany for a way out of this bleak situation. Germany came up with a very successful training and career model, the Vocational Education and Training (VET) system that is highly regarded and greatly utilised by the youth.

VET entails a dual vocational training system, with full-time vocational schools as well as universities of applied sciences. Both are very popular, with dual education highly preferred. This unique model combines theory with on-the-job training; young people attend classes while gaining valuable work experience. Enrolments for vocational qualifications are so high in Germany that 349 programmes are offered in dual VETs (Hoeckel & Schwartz, 2010). This is not surprising as the qualifications obtained in the VET colleges offer numerous career options and are flexible enough to be adapted to a continuously changing labour market. This was one of the calls from students protesting in South African TVET colleges in early 2017. They demanded institutions capable of delivering relevant curriculums and knowledge.

The students protesting at the TVET colleges in the 2015 student movements called for adequate tuition funding. Again, the German model could be useful for South Africa: there is both public and private funding for VETS with both state and private colleges. Perhaps the most important lesson South Africa can take from German VET colleges is that if the majority of our country's workforce received their qualifications in TVET colleges, South Africa would be closer to the NDP dream of massive industrialisation.

Decolonising TVET institutions

I contend that decolonisation of the higher education sector must include a transformation in the idea and concepts we have about what education is, that an entire shift in the importance skills institutions such as TVET colleges be made. The low priority accorded to TVET colleges, to the extent that they are labelled 'alternative' education, is contributing to the crisis facing higher education and is mired in colonial thinking. The thinking that there are forms of learning which are considered more important, relevant and respectable than others is not going to lift South Africa from the grips of absolute poverty.

TVET colleges are already meeting one of the calls from students at traditional universities. The rallying slogan used by students at public universities is 'Free, Quality and Decolonised Education'. TVETs are already doing well in providing NSFAS funding at these public colleges, which covers 80% of all TVET students.

The most important outcome of vocational education is that it should increase students' chances of getting a job or of being self-sustaining entrepreneurs. TVET colleges should be in a position to produce skilled students that play a role in economic expansion and progressive growth. However, the challenge is that these TVET institutions do not always have the resources they need to offer quality technical and vocational training. It is up to our government to change this. But support from industry and the private sector is also badly needed.

Employers in South Africa's developing economy should not have difficulty recruiting skilled labour. The narrative led by the government, endorsed by the youth, needs to change from a focus on mass enrolment at universities towards an emphasis on more diverse higher education such as TVET colleges. The South African economy could do with fewer Bachelor of Arts graduates but more skilled and qualified electricians, mechanics or plumbers etc.

Free education of December 2017

The fee-free higher education announcement by former president Jacob Zuma in December 2017 speaks volumes about the goals government has for TVET colleges. There is now a sense that government takes seriously the idea of fully developing the TVET sector to full capacity especially since there is an objective to produce 30 000 artisans each year until 2030 (President's Statement, 2017). Evidence from across the globe suggests that skills gained from these colleges certainly power the economy. The President's Statement (2017) committed to:

- Giving full bursary support for tuition and study materials to poor but qualifying students at TVET colleges
- Providing fully subsidised free education and training to poor and working-class students at all public TVET colleges starting in 2018
- Funding the studies of all poor and working-class South African students enrolled at public TVET colleges through grants not loans
- Providing for TVET colleges the full cost of study, which will include tuition fee, prescribed study material, meals, accommodation and/or transport
- The government further investing in the training and development of existing TVET staff and the recruitment of additional qualified staff to improve the quality of teaching and learning at TVET colleges.
- Funds being directed towards the improvement of infrastructure in the TVET sector.

Conclusion
South African parents as well as students and learners need to appreciate that vocational skills development is central to creating jobs, entrepreneurship and an inclusive economy for all. Government needs to find creative ways of marketing the TVET sector of higher education better, to give it more prestige and to make it more appealing to young people leaving high school. The president's announcement on fee-free higher education speaks wonderfully on plans for the TVET sector. It is important that we support government and stay positive so as to ensure there is real change, not just the appearance of commitment by government. At the same time, it is important that students that attend these institutions keep putting pressure on government to prioritise and not ignore them. The anger we share

about the status quo can be a useful driver for the youth to strive for excellence not only through universities but also by following the TVET path. Perhaps this could be the answer to the radical economic transformation the government talks of today. And yes, the big issue is where funding for the sector will come from especially as it is severely under-resourced while attracting the most marginalised of the segment of our population.

References
Department of Higher Education and Training. (2013). Fact Sheet on NEETs: An Analysis of the 2011 South African Census. Pretoria, South Africa

Statistics South Africa. (2017). Quarterly Labour Force Survey. Quarter 1: 2017. Pretoria, South Africa

OECD. 2017. *OECD Employment Outlook 2017*, OECD Publishing, Paris. Available at: http://dx.doi.org/10.1787/empl_outlook-2017-en. Accessed on 17 October 2018.

Hoeckel, K. & R. Schwartz, R. 2010. 'Learning for jobs: OECD reviews of vocational education and training', OECD Working Paper, OECD, Germany.

Qubeka, X. 2017. Overcoming our Past. IOL Business Report. 5 May 2017. Available at: https://www.iol.co.za/business-report/opinion/overcoming-our-past-8965822. Accessed 24 April 2017.

The Presidency. 2017. The presidents response to the Heher Commission of Inquiry into Higher Education and Training. Available at: http://www.thepresidency.gov.za/press-statements/president%E2%80%99s-response-heher-commission-inquiry-higher-education-and-training. Accessed on 05 November 2018.

The shared lessons of our liberation history: Placing the Congress Youth League in the struggle for #FeesMustFall in South Africa

Asanda Luwaca

ONE OF THE MOST STRIKING features of the African polity in pre-liberation struggle was the ability of youth formations to radically reshape the methods of struggle against oppressive regimes. A commonality with these liberation movements is the important and historic role that young people played, both in the processes of political and economic transformation under the liberation movements and the processes that followed after political power was seized and state apparatus was occupied (or, in the case of South Africa, since the first democratic general elections).

The youth of the People's Movement for the Liberation of Angola (MPLA), for instance, founded in 1956, was seen as the 'hotbed of the MPLA liberation movement of Angola' (MPLA, 2018). This youth wing was a dynamic force that mobilised the youth to fight against the regime and assumed the moral as well as the political education of young people.

The South West Africa People's Organisation of Namibia (SWAPO) put out a number of publications in exile, which had served as the 'principle medium of agitation politics and instruments for the inculcation of the nationalist sentiments' (Heuva, 2003: 25). Some of these messages, which were ideologically charged messages carried out in these publications, were produced under, and put out, by the auspices of the SWAPO Youth League (SYL).

On the eastern front, in order to fight the Portuguese and liberate Mozambique, the Mozambique Liberation Front (FRELIMO) leaders wanted to foster the revolutionary potential of disgruntled Mozambican youths who had arrived in Tanzania as refugees in the late 1950s and early 1960s. Often arriving impoverished, orphaned and malnourished but burning with the passion of toppling the oppressive state, many of these youths sought retribution against the racist and exploitative policies of Portuguese colonialism. FRELIMO, with its promises of social and political emancipation, offered an attractive alternative to the youth. These young people declared war on the Portuguese as either soldiers on the frontlines or as students attending the FRELIMO secondary school at the Mozambique Institute.

In South Africa, there were growing tensions and mounting calls for militancy and passive resistance against the oppressive apartheid regime. In response to this, a group of young activists, made up of Anton Lembede, Ashby Peter Mda and Jordan Ngubane, wrote a draft manifesto in 1944, which was highly critical of the African National Congress (ANC) leadership. In this manifesto, the group expressed their frustrations in this manner: 'We attribute the inability of Congress in the last twenty years to advance the national cause in a manner commensurate with the demands of the time, to weakness in the organisation and constitution; to its erratic policy of yielding to oppression. Regarding itself as a body of gentlemen with clean hands and to failing to see the problems of the African through proper perspective' (Glaser, 2013: 29). Through various consultative processes that took place within the organisation, a decision was taken in favour of the formation of the African National Congress Youth League (ANCYL) in 1944. The ANCYL was formed to supplement, consolidate and give impetus to the struggle against racial oppression as championed by the ANC. An emphasis was placed on advancing the ideological position of African nationalism, which reaffirmed the role of Africans as their own liberators within the country as well as abroad. Through this ideology, the ANCYL was able to advance its programme of action, which was later adopted by the ANC conference of 1949, which gave rise to the Defiance Campaign – a starting point which would later result in toppling the apartheid regime.

The struggle took on a different direction from the 1960s when the ANC was banned and the ANCYL ceased to exist as an open, mass-based organisation. Despite this era that can be characterised by political inactivity, young people inside the country as well as in exile were at the forefront of the struggle against the oppressive regime. Most battles inside the country at the time were led by young people: National Union of South African Students (NUSAS), South African Students' Organisation (SASO), South African Students Movement (SASM), the 1976 generation, Congress of South African Students (COSAS), South African Youth Congress (SAYCO) as well as other youth formations. In the 1980s when President Oliver Tambo urged all progressive forces to make the country ungovernable, it was due to the bravery of young activists who heeded that call in the face of harassment and repression that earned them the title of 'Young Lions'.

Throughout historical tales of African liberation, the voice of the youth has always been heard and their vibrancy and militant stance against colonial rule continues to inspire the youth of today. In the words of one of the South Africa's liberation icons, O. R. Tambo, 'the children of any nation are its future. A country, a movement, a person that does not value its youth and children does not deserve its future.'

The results of the Quarterly Labour Force Survey (QLFS) for the third quarter of 2017 released by Statistics South Africa indicate that the youth (15–34 years) unemployment rate was 38.6% which is 10.9% above the national average. The same report further indicated that 'of the 10.3 million young persons aged 15–24 years, about 30% were not in employment, education or training'. These high levels of unemployment amongst the youth and lack of access to education or training in the country are intricately linked to the historical injustices that placed access to quality education in favour of the minority group, while the majority black population was left on the peripheral margins.

According to Dewey (1916: 3), education is the 'means of the social continuity of life'. Thus education, in and of itself, becomes a means for expedient mobility and serves as an agency for socio-economic emancipation. The importance of free and quality education has historically been the political vision of the ANCYL. In 1948, the

Youth League had already begun to affirm this position. They stated:

> The ultimate goal of African nationalism, insofar as education is concerned, is a 100 per cent literacy among the people, in order to ensure the realisation of an effective democracy. One of the means to attain this is to ensure free compulsory education for all children, with its concomitants of adequate accommodation, adequate training facilities and adequate remuneration for teachers (ANC Youth League basic policy document, 1948: 2).

Throughout history, the ANCYL has consistently called for the reduction of the financial burden on poor students to pursue higher education. At the 1998 20th National Conference it called for increased funding for the National Student Financial Aid Scheme (NSFAS) through contributions from government, local and foreign donors as well as from the private sector. The call was echoed at the 23rd National Conference (2008). In short, the ANCYL saw affordable education as critical to the realisation of the call for 'People's Education for People's Power'. The League thus supported the call for free education and to see its implementation further resolved to intensify the free education campaign. It was the ANCYL that noted that young people face a complex conundrum: they cannot access employment opportunities because they lack necessary skills and experience, but simultaneously face serious obstacles in accessing skills due to the high cost of post-matric education and weaknesses in the further education and training (FET) and workplace-learning stream. It was at this point that the ANCYL made a clarion call for the de-commodification of the education system, moving from the premise that education should be a right for all and not for the privileged few. This view gained traction as it was asking for a move away from a class commodification of education, where those who could afford it are given quality education and those who cannot afford it receive below-standard education, to a more egalitarian approach where no young person would be denied their right to quality education, irrespective of their socio-economic position in society.

The frustrations of the Youth League began to mount in early 2012 when it threw its support behind the nationwide mass action organised by the South African Students Congress (SASCO). These two organisations, forming part of the Progressive Youth Alliance (PYA), were marching against the exclusionary nature of institutions of higher learning, where the majority of young people were being denied access. These two youth formations called for the immediate implementation of the resolutions taken in the 2007 Polokwane Conference of the ANC – a resolution which had, up until the announcement made by former President Jacob Zuma in December 2017, been in a perpetual state of reaffirmation conference after conference. Since 1955, the South African society and the PYA have always articulated access to higher education as attainable through state allowances and that 'education shall be free, compulsory, universal and equal for all children' – as per the Freedom Charter.

The ANC's 2007 conference policy resolution says: 'Free higher education for the poor up to undergraduate level shall be introduced progressively.' However, the ANC, in its delay in implementing its own decisions, further exacerbated an already fragile crisis.

The events that transpired from 2015 onwards reshaped youth and student politics and virtually displaced the Congress Youth League to a state of capitulation. What became known as the #FeesMustFall movement across the country, where students from institutions of higher learning embarked on mass protests calling for fee-free education, later became the foundation for which government would fast-track the process of legislating free education. A momentous epoch in recent history of South Africa reaffirmed the ability of young people to reshape a society that would be characterised by a shared vision and a collective goal.

But unfortunately, history will remember these events as one where there was an absence of ANCYL leadership in addressing these issues. This was a period that was very different from that of the early 1940s, when ANCYL leaders challenged the senior leadership of the ANC and ultimately reshaped the ANC towards radicalism and militancy. As Joel Netshitenzhe said in 2017, speaking about the ANC's Strategy and Tactics document ahead of the ANC Policy Conference in 2017, 'the Youth League is faced with a similar opportunity, but instead of being the Mandelas and Tambos of our time, they have become foot soldiers of factionalism' (Cele, 2017).

It is undeniable that those who were at the forefront of these mass protests were indeed members and leaders of the ANCYL in their respective institutions of higher learning. But if one has to look at the collective leadership of the ANCYL throughout this movement, one begins to establish the presence of a lacuna in the role that the ANCYL leadership played while all these events transpired. This, unfortunately, was allowed to happen because of the absence of decisive leadership and the presence of factional battles within the ANCYL, which then led them to ignore their twin-tasked mandate of championing the interests of young people and mobilising young people under the banner of the ANC.

Instead of garnering support for the #FeesMustFall movement, the incumbent leadership of the ANCYL distanced itself from it and further called on the country's intelligence agencies to probe the movement, claiming that it was part of a 'counter-revolutionary' movement bent on overthrowing the government (Cele, 2016). The Youth League president went on to make frivolous claims questioning the funding of this movement and how it drew parallel with the then spate of racial incidents.

The president of the ANCYL at the time had also reportedly drawn parallels between the #FeesMustFall movement and the rising scourge of racism in the country. 'The #FeesMustFall campaign and racism – it is all one thing and has the intent to overthrow a democratically elected government of the people' (Cele, 2016).

The announcement made by former president Jacob Zuma on free tertiary education being available for learners who come from households earning an annual income below R350 000 has been misdirected to the ANCYL. The League claims to be the success behind this announcement, claiming to have lobbied the ANC leading up to its 2017 National Elective Conference to make the ultimate decision to make education free for poor students in the 2018 academic year but very little is mentioned on what it did to ensure that the policy gets implemented.

No consultations took place; organisationally, no Branch General Meetings (BGMs) were convened by the leadership to ascertain the position of branches on this subject matter so as to establish the policy position of the ANCYL leading up to the Conference as per standard procedure of the organisation.

In fact, the only mention of this subject that the ANCYL submitted as part of their 2017 conference perspective was that the conference must take a resolution to declare a crisis in South African higher education. This, they argued, must include an instruction to cabinet to urgently deal with the shortage of accommodation, the shortage of enrolment space and the high costs of tuition.

When assessing the resolutions taken by the ANCYL in its National Conference of 2015 and the pronouncement of free education by the ANC in its 2017 National Conference, one picks up inconsistencies. For starters, the Youth League resolved to 'progressively introduce free and compulsory education post-matric' (2015: 46). This resolution alone has no sense of urgency and rigour that has been displayed in past resolutions.

Moreover, the resolution seems to place the Youth League as a somewhat passive participant with no active role and influence to exert pressure on its mother body, the ANC, to fast-track the implementation of free education, as has been the historic position of the ANCYL. Instead, it is portrayed as a 'by the way' statement that has been put in the resolutions as a means of rubber stamping the historic position of the Youth League.

The leadership of the ANCYL remained indifferent when students were fighting for free quality decolonised education. They remained silent even in cases where the struggles were led by members of the PYA such as SASCO and COSAS who share offices with the ANCYL at the ANC headquarters in Johannesburg. They did not support their own members who led protests at Wits university and elsewhere. This was at a time when going against the mother body (ANC) seemed unpopular across the Mass Democratic Movement. Yet today the ANCYL wants to claim easy victories at the expense of those students who faced exclusion from their institutions of higher learning and prison sentences for their involvement in the illegal protests. The leadership of the ANCYL did not show up to some of the trials of the student protests. In some instances, these students were represented by members of opposition political parties.

There has been not a single event in the history of the country involving a youth matter in which the ANCYL and its leadership were not seen or heard. Historical records can attest that even in post-liberation South Africa, the voice of the ANCYL has always served as a catalyst for transformation: from its role played in dismantling the self-defence units (which were formed in 1991 by the ANC at the height of township violence between the ANC and IFP supporters) (Rakgoadi, 1995) to the setting up of organisations like the National

Youth Commission and the Umsobomvu Youth Fund (later became the National Youth Development Agency), the National Youth Trade Investment Corporation, Lembede Investment Holdings to name just a few.

The monumental role of South African youth in the fight against apartheid can never be disputed. The new dispensation has necessitated the youth to, once again, occupy the centre stage of transformation in all spheres of life, particularly towards the realisation of free education. If the Youth League is to be honest with itself, then it will first have to admit that it cannot claim victory over the realisation of free education.

If anything, the League has been, on a number of occasions, caught flat-footed in recent years in its inability to serve as an ally for all youth and the youth organisations during the fees protests. There is a dire need for the ANCYL to go back to its older character and profile of leading the masses from the front, and especially to re-organise, re-align and re-commit itself to selflessly serving the true interests of young people.

It is essential for the ANCYL to revive, rescue and re-organise itself in the changing form and nature of a post-apartheid South Africa. Firstly, it needs to revive its rightful character insofar as its vibrancy and progressive militancy are concerned. By this I mean it needs to go back to its grassroots, the basic unit of the organisation, and spearhead impact-driven programmes that will conscientise young people and change the material conditions that the majority of young people find themselves in.

This revival cannot happen in the absence of re-instilling its twin tasks of championing the interests of young people and mobilising young people under the banner of the ANC. This revival needs to take place by active measures being taken by the League to re-establish its legitimacy, discipline and autonomy, free from political influence and coercion by its parent body. The period of 2012–2022 was marked as that of 'The Decade of the Cadre' where ANC members are called to mobilise, engage with communities and rebuild structures.

This attribute needs to be reflected in the League and internalised and not used as meaningless rhetoric and sloganeering. It is worth noting that history has no blank pages and that it was in 2012 that the ANCYL pronounced a programme of action for the realisation of 'Economic Freedom in our Lifetime'. With the staggering levels of unemployment, predominantly among the youth, the ANCYL should revive this level of political consciousness it once had and selflessly defend this clarion call as one which was resolved by ANCYL members in Conference, and not create a vacuum for opposition to claim it as a programme of individuals.

Secondly, the ANCYL needs to rescue itself from the bondages of the dependency relationship it has with the ANC. The establishment of the ANCYL was founded on the principle of the self-determination of the African nation but that character has withered away over the recent years. The ANCYL has always been a highly contested terrain of influence by the ANC, but the League has never caved in to the influence of the ANC. In fact, the ANCYL has always had an influence in the ANC and not the other way around. The key to this lies in its autonomous nature – the right to self-govern.

And lastly, the ANCYL needs to re-organise itself for some genuine organisational rebuilding so that it becomes visible in the election work of the ANC (as it is the ANC that contests elections after all and not the Youth League). It needs to rally the increasingly growing youth populace behind the ANC, whilst still advancing youth development. It needs to also re-organise itself towards building a second layer of leadership that is not only politically, but academically capable, in line with what is required of a people working towards the realisation of a national democratic society. It needs to re-organise itself in that it may be capable of uniting the PYA and all other youth formations and/or youth movements across the country. Synergy between these structures is paramount in order to adequately regain support and confidence among the youth.

References

ANC 52nd National Conference resolutions. 2007. Available at: http://www.anc.org.za/content/52nd-national-conference-resolutions. Accessed on 31 January 2018.

ANC Youth League 23rd National Congress resolutions. 2008. Available at: http://www.ancyl.org.za/show.php?id=5485. Accessed on 1 February 2018.

ANC Youth League 25th National Congress report. 2015. Available at: www.ancyl.org.za/docs/reps/2015/congress-report.pdf. Accessed on 3 February 2018.

ANC Youth League basic policy document. 1948. Available at: www.ancyl.org.za/docs/political/1948/ANC%20Youth%20League%20Basic%20Policy%20Documentk.pdf. Accessed on 31 January 2018.

Cele, S. 2016. '#FeesMustFall is treason'. *City Press*, 31 January. Available at: http://city-press.news24.com/News/ancyl-leader-feesmustfall-is-treason 20160131?utm_content=buffer89b3f&utm_medium=social&utm_

source=facebook.com&utm_campaign=buffer. Accessed on 17 January 2018.
Cele, S. 2017. 'Netshitenzhe berates ANC Youth League'. *City Press*, 10 June. Available at: http://city-press.news24.com/News/netshitenzhe-berates-anc-youth-league-20170610. Accessed on 17 January 2018.
Dewey, J. 1916. *Education and Democracy: An Introduction to the Philosophy of Education*. New York: Macmillan.
Freedom Charter. 1955. Historical papers research archive, Johannesburg. Available at: http://www.historicalpapers.wits.ac.za/inventories/inv_pdfo/AD1137/AD1137-Ea6-1-001-jpeg.pdf. Accessed on 04 November 2018.
Glaser, C. 2012. *The ANC Youth League*. Johannesburg: Jacana Media.
Godlimpi, Z 2017. Policy conference pamphlet. [email].
Heuva, W. 2003. 'Voices in the liberation struggle', in H. Melber, ed. *Re-examining Liberation in Namibia: Political Culture Since Independence*. Uppsala: Nordic Africa Institute.
MPLA. 2018. 'Historia'. Available at: http://www.mpla.ao/jmpla.39/historia.40.html. Accessed on 29 January 2018.
Rakgoadi, S. 1995. 'The role of the self-defense units (SDUs) in a changing political context'. Available at: http://www.csvr.org.za/publications/latest-publications/1466-the-role-of-the-self-defence-units-sdus-in-a-changing-political-context. Accessed on 3 February 2018.
Statistics South Africa. 2017. *Quarterly Labour Force Survey – QLFS Q3: 2017*. Available at: http://www.statssa.gov.za/?p=10658. Accessed on 15 February 2018.

Why the EFF is gaining ground at South African universities: A post #FeesMustFall legacy

Wandile Ngcaweni

IT IS NOW WELL KNOWN HOW successful the Economic Freedom Fighters Students Command (EFFSC) has been in the 2016/2017 student representative council (SRC) elections in several universities across the country. They have scored victories at Wits, Limpopo, Sefako Makgatho and other universities, even at TVET colleges. There is an on-going debate about why the EFFSC is becoming popular and gaining ground amongst students and therefore SRC elections in South Africa's tertiary institutions.

Eight points to ignite the debate
1. Kardashianomics (conspicuous consumption and narcissism) as defined elsewhere by Busani Ngcaweni preoccupies some of the popular Progressive Youth Alliance (PYA) leaders. The PYA has been slow to shrug off perceptions that its leaders are not genuinely concerned about the plight of poor students. Allegations of using access to power and resources go on for months unchallenged. This spreads the image of leaders preoccupied with themselves, conspicuous consumption and popularity. These widespread perceptions could be built on residual effects of macro social dynamics or they

are merely a microcosm of national political elite formation. It worries us in the congress movement when PYA leaders are seen to be chasing the good life and not prioritising the general welfare of students. Many times, during the Fees Must Fall protests, we heard allegations of PYA leaders receiving bribes from ANC proxies like Shaka Sisulu in return for them urging students to stop the protests. Perceptions are much more powerful than actual evidence especially in an unsympathetic social media environment. The EFFSC, on the other hand, deals harshly with those seen to be leading flashy lifestyles. While their commander-in-chief loves Gucci and other top brands licensed to the Stellenbosch-based godfather of white monopoly capital (Johann Rupert), its student command is never seen as flashy. In the PYA, the margin of tolerance of conspicuous consumption is unlimited. One needs only to attend one of their campus parties to see the premium vodka and whisky these young lions consume sometimes at the cost of the SRC allowances given by the university. It is part of the body politic of the broader movement. Even to campaign for the SRC you hear young comrades say 'we need resources chief...'

2. The PYA, in the campuses they have lost both elections, has arguably created a social distance between itself and the students they lead, much like the parent movement – the ANC. The overall feeling is that under the PYA, the student struggles have moved to boardroom discussions at a time when students on the ground are facing challenges that require street politics. The EEFSC capitalised on this by using radical rhetoric and their readiness to show agency by taking to the streets and breaking a window or two. This appeals to students who think SRCs can sometimes make too many compromises with management in these boardroom meetings. For its part, the PYA's mother body has recognised the need to reconnect with the electorate in order to close the social distance which affects electoral outcomes. Even Parliament has become more active in recent times in an attempt to regain legitimacy in the eyes of the impatient public.

3. Radical and populist posturing have begun to appeal to students who have suffered for so long in what is now overwhelmingly considered a neo-liberal arrangement whereby there has been no qualitative transformation to cure the wounds of apartheid colonialism. Hence the movement now argues for radical economic transformation to fast-track socio-economic inclusion. The EFFSC exploited this gap. They have been uncompromising on what their goals for society look like – hence the coincidence of their land policies and students' calls for free, quality and decolonised higher education. This radical rhetoric has appealed to students who do not want to wait for transformation to come some day. Again, breaking windows and flooding libraries is seen to be the language that authorities listen to more, thus forcing them to act quicker.
4. The EFF has branded itself (ideologically and symbolically) as an alternative to the PYA. Inequality as a perceived or lived experience of black students at UCT, VUT, CPUT and at Wits for example, shapes students' perspective away from the ruling party (ANC) and SASCO in particular who are seen to be content with a status quo where poverty, inequality and epistemic exclusion prevails. What else could explain the EFF Student Command winning 12 out 15 seats at the 2017/2018 Wits SRC elections?
5. Arrogance of management goes a long way towards radicalising students. Importantly, this arrogance also manifested in the bullying of the PYA leadership who have been undermined by unilateral decisions of governing structures. Students react to this bullying by supporting those ready to break bones and flood/burn libraries in retaliation. Wits is a case point. Just look at how Mcebo Dlamini and Nompendulo were treated by management at Wits – no different to how student leaders where treated by apartheid university administrators.
6. Social media has opened intellectual spaces thus helping students re-discover Pan-Africanist and Black Consciousness literature (ideas and leaders) which have been 'hidden' from the curriculum and mainstream political

discourse. This 're-discovery' of Biko, Fanon, Sankara and Sobukwe is shaping popular ideas and those seen to be inspired by these ideas are appealing to the students. The Wits PYA backing out of a campus debate with the EFFSC on the eve of the SRC elections outed them as intellectual cowards with no intellectual stamina, political theory and consciousness. A fatal mistake.

7. The successes of the 2015/16 #RhodesMustFall and #FeesMustFall campaigns are the crown jewels of radical, populist and Africanist student movements. They won concessions in two years which tertiary education elites had resisted for 20 years. Suddenly, every university began removing colonial symbols, changing curriculums, recognising black and female scholars, in-sourcing security and cleaning services etc. More importantly, like Rhodes, fees have 'fallen' for all poor and lower middle-class students. The EFFSC claims this as an incomplete victory and therefore continues to mobilise students while the PYA are being undermined by its leaders who lie on the issue of decolonised quality higher education. In the September 2018 round of SRC elections, the EFFSC has had convincing victories in many universities in South Africa including clean sweeps at tradionally SASCO strongholds such as Mangosuthu University of Technology, Durban University of Technology, University of Zululand, University of the Free State as well as the Mafikeng Campus of North-West University. Something needs be said too about previous Democratic Alliance Student Organisation (DASO) wins as well. For the purpose of this essay, we will call these wins 'right turns' or circumstances under which students previously voted for right-wing parties. Who can forget the near-recent scandalous DASO victory at Fort Hare, coinciding with the university's jubilee celebrations? With the EFFSC making inroads in the past two to three years, we are now seeing 'left turns' in SRCs gaining ground as a push back against rising inequality, democratic indifference and colonialism.

8. As the EFF continues to capture the national imagination

and to grow in influence, so are the fortunes trickling to its student commands. They are seen to be speaking truth to power and being true champions of poor students. They have created an image of themselves as an organisation created to serve the people and challenge black poverty and deprivation. They are directly taking on white arrogance and reaffirming black self-worth. This is vital in that the students' conditions are seen as a consequence of political economy, not an isolated incidence of campus life. On the other hand, the PYA has largely been focused on campus politics, partly because of the apathy of its leader, the ANC Youth League. I will not venture into what is to be done because everyone knows what ought to be done by the movement to reassert the hegemony of the PYA in order for SASCO to lead students at campus and national levels. Also, the age-old debate of the Youth League contesting SRC elections has to be decisively addressed. In the meantime, #FeesMustFall protests of 2017 have commenced in various universities across the country yet again. This time the student leadership political landscape has drastically changed. The EFFSC's agenda continues to win the hearts and minds of students across provinces and campuses across the country.

Aryan Kaganof's *Decolonising Wits*: A film analysis

Azola Dayile

THROUGHOUT MODERN HUMAN existence, certain bodies have been rendered null and void – only fit as objects for scientific research and experimentation and as hyper-sexualised objects for sexual gratification and/or entertainment. These 'othered' bodies – if seen through Gramsci's notion of hegemony and Althusser's concept of ideological state apparatus – are created, produced and reproduced by dominant bodies. These wield power through their collective hegemony over the ideological state apparatus, made up of the family, schools and universities as well as the church and the media, which all function to create the realm of ideology. In contemporary post-apartheid South Africa, the film industry – along with the mainstream media industry – contributes to the maintenance and perpetuation of a set of power relations that grants the dominant bodies the power to create, produce and reproduce the 'Other' in their own conception and desire, through multiple avenues including (mis)representation, which is the dominant method of othering by those who have the power to control the media.

There has been an emergence of new left-wing student movements on university and college campuses around the country. These were formed to combat racial discrimination and the commodification of education, and to try and establish an education system that truly humanises those who have had their humanity violently stripped since the earliest days of slavery .

University grounds and lecture halls became sites of struggle and thus student protests broke out as a result. At the University of the Witwaterstrand (Wits), the students – under the leadership of the Economic Freedom Fighters Students Command (EFFSC) – mobilised and organised protests that eventually led to a meeting with the top management, led by Vice Chancellor Professor Adam Habib.

Filmmaker Aryan Kaganof was there with them almost every step of the way, together with his camera capturing the saga and emotions as they unfolded. The footage from the Wits encounter between the students and senior management became what is now a documentary film titled *Decolonising Wits* (2015), produced and directed by Kaganof himself. In what follows, the film shall be critically engaged with in terms of its depiction of how education in post-apartheid South Africa has been made exclusive through the neo-liberal pressures of privatisation and exclusionary school policies, based on race, class, gender and/or sexual orientation, curriculum content and pedagogy.

I intend to, firstly, provide a synopsis of the film. Secondly, I shall look at how these forms of power-for-oppression and exclusion are maintained and subsequently challenged in the film. Lastly, I shall render a critique of the film for how it also contributes to and reproduces capitalism and anti-blackness.

The feature-length documentary film, *Decolonising Wits* (2015), follows the lives of a group of politically charged black students at the University of the Witwaterstrand, as they navigate their way through student politics (as a tool of resistance) and grapple with questions of black alienation and capitalist exploitation at the university, through practices such as the hiking of fees, outsourcing and racial discrimination – both at the level of epistemology and pedagogy. The film radically challenges generally accepted mainstream filmmaking conventions, subverting them in an attempt to capture the event under consideration.

In the film, the EFFSC initiates a process of mobilising and organising black students of Wits university into confronting the institutional power embodied by the head of the institution, Professor Adam Habib. The gripe the students have with the university – and by extension the post-apartheid 'rainbow' nation state – is because of the slow pace of transformation, or rather decolonisation as the

Above: Students from the University of Johannesburg chant and sing struggle songs outside the Brixton Police Station to demand the release of about 140 of their fellow students who were arrested during a Fees Must Fall protest. This was on 16 November 2015. (Photo: Paballo Thekiso)

Below: University of Cape Town (UCT) students in a confrontation with members of the South Africa Police Service during the Fees Must Fall shutdown protest at UCT on 7 November 2017. (Photo: Wandile Kasibe)

Above: Former Wits university SRC president and activist Mcebo Dlamini addresses students at the Wits Concourse during the #FeesMustFall gathering on 16 October 2015. Universities were shut down for weeks as students protested and demanded free education be implemented in universities. (Photo: Paballo Thekiso)

Below: Wits EFF Student Command leader Vuyani Pambo speaks to Wits university Vice Chancellor Adam Habib and his team inside the Great Hall where students refused to let him leave until their demands of free education and other concerns were resolved. This took place on 16 October 2015. (Photo: Paballo Thekiso)

Above: Police surround a student after spraying him with pepper spray in an effort to disperse students who had gathered outside Luthuli House in Joburg CBD to deliver a memorandum to the ANC demanding free education across the country. This happened on 22 October 2015. (Photo: Paballo Thekiso)

Below: University of Cape Town (UCT) students being manhandled by Vetus Schola private security during a campus shutdown protest at UCT Lower Campus on 17 October 2016. (Photo: Wandile Kasibe)

Above: A student holds a placard during the Fees Must Fall protest on 30 September 2016 opposing the University of Cape Town reopening on 3 October 2016. (Photo: Wandile Kasibe)
Below: Fees Must Fall protest at Parliament during the Budget Vote speech on 21 October 2015 demanding free decolonised education. (Photo: Wandile Kasibe)

Above: Students from various universities gathering at the Union Buildings demanding free education on 23 October 2015. (Photo: Menzi Mkhize)

Below: Students surround their fellow comrade and try to calm him down with milk after he inhaled teargas from the police who tried to disperse students. The students had gathered outside Luthuli House in Joburg CBD to deliver a memorandum to the ANC demanding free education across the country. This happened on 22 October 2015. (Photo: Paballo Thekiso)

Above: The removal of the statue of Cecil John Rhodes from its plinth at the centre of the University of Cape Town on 9 April 2015. (Photo: Wandile Kasibe)

Below: Kgotsi Chikane being arrested during the Fees Must Fall protest at Parliament on 21 October 2015. (Photo: Wandile Kasibe)

Above: Students hold placards and stand around candles outside Brixton Police Station after over 140 of their fellow students and some employees were detained over protests about the outsourcing of cleaning and security personnel at the University of Johannesburg. This took place on 11 November 2015. (Photo: Paballo Thekiso)

Below: A student holds a placard with the inscription '1976 reloaded' during a Fees Must Fall protest at Parliament on 21 October 2015. (Photo: Wandile Kasibe)

Above: 'Free Education' graffiti is seen on Ntemi Piliso street in Joburg CBD after students from surrounding universities marched and demanded free education across the country's universities. This happened on 22 October 2015. (Photo: Paballo Thekiso)

Below: A woman wearing a t-shirt with the 'Free Education Now' slogan stands raising her fist as a salute to the late struggle icon Winnie Madikizela-Mandela. Thousands of people put flowers outside her house in Orlando West, Soweto upon her passing. (Photo: Paballo Thekiso)

students correctly term it, evinced in the exploitative outsourcing of essential support services such as cleaning, safety and security, as well as grounds maintenance at Wits university.

In their struggle for recognition from a sympathetic ally and an ear to listen to them, the students insist that Habib – as a former student leader himself and credible social scientist – should assume the role of ally. However, he decides to align himself instead with the oppressive bureaucratic administration of the university. In the students' resistance against the multiple forms of power that seek to make them invisible (even in their physical presence), amaGwijo – traditional songs of struggle – become a morale booster and a reminder to all of the need to struggle. One such Gwijo is 'Biko Wethu gwijo', which is sang as early as four minutes into a film, where the students are likening the contemporary student protests with those of 1976, guided by the Black Consciousness idea/ideal made popular by Steve Biko.

The belief of the students is that the spirit of Biko and his Black Consciousness philosophy would guide them through the struggle to victory, as it did with the youth of 1976 who struggled for the fall of Bantu Education, and subsequently, the entire apartheid regime. The entire film becomes this intertwined web of sequential frames forming a montage that seeks to present a struggle with no linear plot or narrative. In its very last minutes, it ends off with a sign stating 'take alternative route to exit', put up at what seems to be an underground shaft in one of the buildings at the university.

In one of the opening scenes of the film, we are introduced to a black male student in an elevator. The student, as a way of propelling the film forward and introducing the viewer to one of the overarching themes of the film, says 'this university must be changed'. This five-worded sentence then becomes the basis of the film where black students, tired of being reduced and locked into a state of liminality, begin questioning the function and logic of the university, before reaching the conclusion that it 'must be changed'.

For many of them, the university represented the go-to place where dreams were said to come true, but upon their arrival they soon come to learn that the place is not a space they are genuinely welcomed in as they are, because they are only 'accepted' once they agree to alter themselves and fit into the model-type student as decided upon by the university. This statement – that Wits must be changed – speaks back directly to this altering moment and questions its logic and desired intent, concluding that it is illogical as it 'others' the black student into a realm of non-being, only to create for it a new subjectivity according to its own sensibilities. Coming to this conclusion, the black students come to the harsh realisation that the university, in its current form and content, is an anti-black and capitalist institution.

Moreover, what is further revealed as an anti-black space/place within the university in the film – and in the reality of contemporary institutions of higher learning in post-apartheid South Africa – is that the student activists and protestors are overwhelmingly black. This is alarming, especially occurring at an English, liberal, historically white institution, where white presence is still substantial.

One is then left to ask the pertinent question: where are white students and what are they pre-occupied with in post-apartheid, non-racial South Africa, besides being behind fancy cameras capturing history as it unfolds? To be listened to, the black student must 'perform', and that too only by themselves through a series of disruptions at the popular, upmarket cafeteria, switching off the lights during a physics lecture, occupying the VC's office or shutting down the university. Student leader Vuyani Pambo of the EFFSC shouts to his comrades, 'This is theatre, we must perform', and indeed, perform they do, for both the institutional power and the white gaze.

In another of the scenes in the film, Mcebo Dlamini – a former Wits university SRC president and member of the ANC-aligned Progressive Youth Alliance – laments how there is a shortage of adequate housing for black students, resulting in homelessness. He notes how white students avoid sharing a room with any other student, worse so if that student is not white.

Addressing students in 2015, Mcebo Dlamini was once quoted as saying that 'we have to start by first looking at the number of white students admitted at this university and how many of them apply for [campus] res[idences]'. This is allowed, he continued, by the university's middle management and administration, at times in-line with school policy, much to the dismay of black students. These racist tendencies prove how anti-blackness conspires against black bodies in white spaces that claim to be non-racial in orientation.

Moreover, this deficit in adequate student accommodation at the university plays directly into the hands of capitalism, as it allows private student housing and accommodation centres to hike rent prices at their whim. Property groups such as South Point – which have monopoly over student accommodation across South Africa – benefit largely from such an arrangement. To secure a single room at any of the Johannesburg-based South Point student accommodation buildings in 2017 cost just above R4 000 per month, with a booking fee of R1 050 which is non-refundable.

Moreover, before a student is allowed to move into their room, they must first provide one month's rent deposit – which is refundable subject to terms and conditions – over a 10-month, fixed lease beginning from 1 February to 30 November. In effect, a student has to pay over R10 000 upfront to South Point, and this does not include catering or electricity costs. It is important to note that South Point largely caters for poor black students, the majority of whom are funded by the National Student Financial Aid Scheme (NSFAS), as well as various bursary schemes from the public and private sector.

In addition to the exorbitant habitation fees that the university students must pay as a result of coalitions between the university, private and public loans/bursary schemes, as well as student accommodation property groups, Wits University itself has amongst the highest tuition fees in the country for an average, undergraduate degree. For instance, to pursue an undergraduate Bachelor of Arts degree, a student has to pay an average tuition fee of between R36 330 and R46 790 for their first year of study.

This, coupled with application and registration fees, accommodation and catering along with books and stationery easily accumulates to over R100 000 for a single year, amounting to about R300 000 for a full three-year degree. This high financial burden of higher education in post-apartheid South Africa is problematised by the black students of Wits university in the film, with the students referring to Section 29 (1) of the Constitution of the Republic of South Africa Act 108 1996, which provides that 'everyone has the right to basic and further education, including adult basic education' as well as the EFF's 4th cardinal pillar which states that 'free quality education, healthcare, houses, and sanitation should be provisioned for all South African citizens in post-apartheid South Africa'.

The students – guided by the Marxist-Leninist and Fanonian ethos – understand very well that this is one tactic used by those who possess hegemony over state apparatuses, particularly that of education, to pick and choose who comes in and out of the university and at what given moment in time. And because it is largely black students who find themselves without accommodation in Johannesburg's suburban areas, they are mainly the ones who must utilise the services of places such as South Point, which are expensive and often times sub-standard for decent human habitation. Once again, this reveals the gruesomeness of neo-liberalism forging an alliance with Wits university's anti-blackness at the institution.

By the same token, the film, wittingly or unwittingly, falls into the trap of advancing pro-capitalist and anti-black notions. That is, after gathering the footage of the black students at Wits university and their confrontation with the institutional power of the vice chancellor, Kaganof worked on and packaged the fragmented frames into a somewhat coherent documentary film, giving it the title it currently holds. After this, the film was set to screen at local film houses, particularly around Gauteng, notably Ster Kinekor and The Bioscope in Johannesburg as early as 3 July 2015.

It is at this point that the film aligns itself with capitalist practices/tendencies that are coupled with notions of anti-blackness. Kaganof, after his adventure of being the eyes through which the black student struggle is seen at, goes on to privatise the experience and sell it to an exclusive audience of middle-class cinema goers in South Africa.

His intentions may not have been malicious or profit-driven, but the principle of 'selling' images of a real people's struggle to a comfortable and privileged class of people, who are oblivious to the students' plight and erroneously (un)critical of their struggle to decolonise Wits, leaves much to be desired.

Nowhere does Kaganof contextualise his reasons for such a move, perhaps as a fundraising tactic to assist students with meals, rent or legal fees. How it is interpreted then is that the filmmaker has – after being allowed to enter a space that prohibited white presence (as a principle adopted by the protesting students) – taken what he has seen there and looked to profit from it. He has taken black pain, liminality and precariousness and sold it to the highest bidders at local cinemas where middle-class folk go for entertainment and to pass the time.

Furthermore, the ontological positionality of Aryan Kaganof as a white filmmaker filming black student struggles at an anti-black institution should be problematised as it compliments and perpetuates anti-blackness. And this is both overtly and implicitly problematised by some of the student protestors in the film when they refuse Kaganof entry into one of their meetings and ask of him to stop filming.

Some even go to extra lengths and charge for Kaganof's camera in the hope of confiscating it due to his refusal to stop filming. This particular scene adequately captures the antagonism between Kaganof's positionality as a white body and that of students as black bodies. His refusal to leave the room, even after being asked to do so by students, reveals a paternalising attitude that – for the students' plight to be seen and taken seriously – he and his camera must be there, even when not welcomed.

It explicitly suggests that for the black to be seen, the white has to be present, and only through the white's eyes can the black be visible. In turn, this refusal by Kaganof to cease filming the students collaborates with the anti-black institutional power of Wits university and reproduces the black students as objects of parasitical white capacities, ranging from absolute and gratuitous violence to ethical projects aimed at 'upgrading' and telling the story of the black students through cinema. This also reveals how Kaganof is (un)aware of his positionality as a white body that is allowed in all-black spaces, even when the blacks themselves reach consensus to prohibit white presence.

This orientation that seeks to maintain anti-blackness is further legitimised by the post-apartheid non-racial state. It allows whites to make false claims that they possess the ethical and productive norms needed to improve black lives in civil society and political economy, as is the case in post-apartheid South Africa (POSTASA). And this justifies the positing of black bodies as objects of white meditation, instruction, concern or coercion as seen with Kaganof and the making of his film.

Even though he is present at every given moment of the students fight with white institutional power, Kaganof can never understand or experience the lived experience of the university's black students. This is not solely because he has a lighter skin colour. It has everything to do with the organisation of the institution and the post-apartheid South African state where anti-blackness operates as a paradigm that imposes social death upon black life, subjectivity and agency. This is how the film and the filmmaker maintain and perpetuate anti-blackness, which operates beyond racial discrimination and socio-economic exploitation and alienation.

The students in their state of liminality – both at the university and in post-apartheid South Africa – navigate the university campus, singing, scheming, mobilising and confronting institutional power to demand change and answers to questions around alienation, homelessness, exorbitant fees and racism. Through this struggle, Kaganof and his camera are present and capturing history as it unfolds. But, as highlighted above, this also plays into the hands of anti-black capitalism through Kaganof's decision, whether the students consented or not, to privatise the film and screen it at bourgeois film houses to a middle-class audience. Further, his positionality as a white male body filming the plight of poor black students at their most vulnerable and refusing to allow them the space to be on their own at such a crucial moment, plays directly into the idea of anti-blackness that suggests the black is no more than an object to be looked at, studied, coerced, silenced and spoken for. In the final analyses, the black students are thought of and constructed as outsiders in a cis-heteronormative, white capitalist and patriarchal institution and film industry.

In conclusion, the film *Decolonising Wits* adequately manages to capture how white institutional power at Wits university, administered by Vice Chancellor Adam Habib, subjugates, 'Others', includes and excludes black bodies through anti-black, pro-capitalist policies that commodify education and coloniality that exists in the university and the contemporary post-apartheid state at large. In having made the film, Kaganof subverts and converts mainstream cinematic expressions and conventions to produce a film that is devoid of a linear plot, narrative and structure. He follows the lives and struggles of a group of black students at university where they mobilise and organise for resistance against an institution that seeks to prey on them through the perpetuation of capitalism and anti-blackness. The students, the majority of whom belong to the EFFSC, come to the realisation that Wits university has to drastically change, and for this change to occur, they themselves have to be the propellant force that will catalyse genuine and sustainable change for the benefit of all marginalised groups at the institution.

PART 2
INTERSECTIONALITY AND FEMINIST PERSPECTIVES

Still hungry

Khanyisile Melanie Mboya

WE WERE FED BUT we were not full,
for there is no worse kind of poverty than one that minimises the portion each time.
Each portion of your history,
each portion of your language,
each portion of your humanity.
We are no longer frustrated by the constipation of our humanity.
Because we have eaten but still we produce no stools,

and so like fools we are told to wander around the untimely aporia of our stools,
with burning ulcers born from sitting still,
But we were born free?
And so, we ate but were never full.
They named us Greedy, Entitled and Lazy but took no notice of our surnames.

Because Greedy was the hungry child of uMsindo.
Waqhawuka ke umsindo ngaloo mini.
Now with a real hunger, a hunger to burn down every single word which had caused them to be malnourished.
Entitled was the child of uBabalwa.
Determined to be counted no matter the few or the many.
Kakade baqala bembalwa.

Lazy was the child of uSiphokazi.
Whose potential was an unfulfilled promise, whose gifts were amputated by false hope.
But as a girl child it was demanded of her;
ukuba avuke abeliqhawekazi, abe yimbokodo yabafazi.
And there was the final child who they thought did not even deserve a name.
The child of uNomalanga.
Who awakened in her hungry siblings the rising sun,
a beam never fading,
a wokeness never sleeping –
an insomniatic cousciousness.
These children are still hungry,
but are fuelled by a petrol that death cannot stop from spreading.
Are lit by a tire that never burns out – even around a human body.
Whose words continuously accumulate so that even the mute will be able to articulate...
'Bahleli bonke etilongweni
Bahleli bonke kwaNongqongqo...'
'Hiyo uSolomon...'
'From Cape to Kairo, Morroco to Margascar, iAzania...'
Gogo, gogo!
Livukile idlozi labantu abatsha, lingqenqgile lilinde kukhwaze izinyanya uba kuyatsha.
This is there food and they will be fed.
These children are still hungry.

The University Currently Known as Rhodes: Reflections from a female student leader

Khanyisile Melanie Mboya

GROWING UP, I WENT to one of those 'former Model C schools' where black students were the majority but most of our teachers were white. Growing up I lived in many homes having to navigate the intricacies of life, the structural and institutional reality of growing up as a black girl. Other times there was the rural hut of my grandmother and others there was the shack we owned and lived in. I also spent time in the garage room, which belonged to my mother's employers. Most of the students at the school I attended navigated and moved between spaces and places, just like most black people still do today – physically by taking a taxi as a way to travel and metaphysically by changing our language and accents, and at times our entire identity as a means to survive. This was a way for us to feel accepted as young people. Memorable experiences at high school include that of my maths teacher who insisted on speaking Afrikaans whenever she was pleased but dare we as African pupils utter sentences in isiXhosa, a demerit was soon to follow as a reminder not to speak 'vernac' in the school. The brave ones would murmur a 'hay' suka uyadika lomama' to which the reply 'Get out of my class!' would often be the response from the teacher.

I remember there was a student in my class who, throughout my schooling career, was never reprimanded if she had not done her homework. This baffled me to the point where I asked, 'Ma'am, Becky hasn't done her homework either, why are you only giving us demerits?' To which she responded, 'I'm not checking homework today anyway, Melanie.' And so, it happened throughout school that if Becky had not done her homework, the whole class's homework would not be checked.

In grade 7, our teachers were recklessly giving us these demerits; I had about 150 by the second term, while most of the others had 100–250 of them, and it took only 10 to get you into Friday detention. That was 15 Fridays gone for me, mostly because I 'talked a lot'; I thought of it as refusing to be told to keep quiet instead!

Looking back, our disobedience was a form of rebellion and protest to unwelcome, often prejudiced, rules and behaviours of our teachers. Even though our methods were highly youthful and ill-advised, we felt we had to push back in that suffocating environment.

At our Matric farewell, without the knowledge of our teachers and some white classmates (because they would tell), we added the song from the movie, *Sarafina*: 'Freedom is coming tomorrow'. Our teachers saw this as a final act of rebellion, but for us it was a celebration – partly for having fought a system but mostly because we had overcome it. We had survived.

Little did we know then and perhaps even less do we know now.

I have since been on the SRC of Rhodes University and have taken part in students' movements across the country, such as #RhodesMustFall, #FeesMustFall and #RUReferenceList. Looking back, I think the work of students within all the movements across the country was the culmination of stories such as these: where our schools, public and private, still reflect who should and should not be in them. Despite the lack of vocabulary for Becky's white privilege and supremacy, the structural violence and racism and finally being so sick and tired that we responded to the injustice as best we knew how. Refusing to be considered misfits we started to understand that the system was not built to fit us, and so as we moved into university we realised the whole damn thing was rotten at best, and self-destructive at its worst. The struggle continued. It has been said and I now understand it personally when older leaders warn that revolutions and struggles of people are never complete.

There have been wins in the movement since 2016 but these are so faint in the face of a monstrous system that has outwardly resisted proposed forms of progress in the journey to transform. There have been wins where women shake mainstream thinking but a loss where the dominant thinking trumps and prevails systematically. When rapists are exposed, women win but they lose when these men are not reprimanded or held accountable, which protects perpetrators and dismisses the pain of these women.

The women of #RUReferenceList have been fighting not just for their education but their livelihood and existence as the University Currently Known as Rhodes (UCKAR) and others push them out of the system and the university institutions using archaic, patriarchal rules and shameful councils and task teams. The harshest blow handed to rape victims and activists in December 2017 was the decision to expel such women and take away the possibility of them to graduate and have degrees. Young women in universities across the country remain unprotected against sexual harassment. Hence, I argue victories are still too far between.

My question has been why is it that the men see themselves first as men then as people and women continue to raise and love them that way?

On Rhodes lecturers

Academics are exceedingly stiff, defensive and often unwilling to engage in anything outside of or unfamiliar with their teaching. The words are transformation, diversity, inclusion. We know them but somehow we cannot realise them. My personal take is that academics are resisters and should just say 'no we don't want to' where they see fit. The only explanation to the slow pace of transformation since the student protests is that they are outright resisting it. So, dear Steve Biko, I don't think the oppressor wants to be free and the work of freeing us both is tiresome.

University management is still calling students 'minority terrorists who hold the innocent hostage'. You cannot negotiate with people who think you are terrorists. Tell us, Mr Madiba, how you did it?

I am interested to engage on how and why we pick and choose social change, where we decide that this is worthy or unworthy. Is Zuma #falling more important than Fees #falling? Is #RUReferenceList more important than queer bodies? Why must we choose at all? South Africa belongs to all who live in it, they say, but somehow only some of us are allowed its full glory. Intersectionality is a concept still misunderstood by many in South Africa and the divisions within student movements also shows that we have failed to give ourselves time to engage with the many progressive concepts we have centred during the 2016 student protests.

Whose voice is going to now be worthy of being listened to? Let us not forget Fort Hare, Walter Sisulu University (WSU), the University of KwaZulu-Natal, and all other historically black universities who protest year-long before they make the news alongside the University of Cape Town (UCT) and Rhodes. Whose voices will be what we need?

With all this colour blindness, who can really see the red lights?

On the role of social media
Social media has been a platform to communicate social change and definitely a necessary public space to override the censoring, lies, propaganda and sensationalism that mainstream news media is ridden with. Nonetheless, social media has become far too often an excuse and safe space to drag and shame others and then log off. You cannot log off when the police start shooting. You cannot edit and backspace your argument to make it more diplomatic when in a moment of rage and absolute frustration you swear at your vice chancellor. And a 'like' on the interdict is not going to make it not go to court. There is a whole world to be dealt with after you log off.

As we move forward as a country, the new academic year will inevitably roll on, various budgets from the universities will be released and new leaders will be elected into various political and bureaucratic positions and so will new SRCs get elected into office in the various universities – Lord help us and them to do right by each other.

I am anxious and concerned that the corner into which marginalised people have been forced leaves them with poor choices; you need only recall how as high school students we replied to resistance to transformation. I do not know what or how we are going to deal with the next wave that is going to be running faster, having run out of patience. They were willing in 1976 but how much more will is in us now and what will it produce?

#PatriarchyMustFall: Tears, complexities and realisations

Annabel Fenton

THE OPPRESSION OF WOMEN is normalised in our current society. We talk about rape on a day-to-day basis without flinching, forgetting the specificity and emotion behind individual experiences. This all changed for me one Wednesday night at Leo Marquard residence, as I stood and listened to women share their stories of being molested as a child, of being publicly shamed by males for being 'ugly', of being called at, and for the first time, I felt like women were able to voice their pain. Tears rolled down my cheeks. It was also a process of realising that so much of what I have experienced – catcalls, fear of rapists on campus that hinder me from walking alone, low self-esteem – is actually symptomatic of a bigger experience of patriarchy in our society. The process of unleashing these stories and emotions affected me deeply over the next few days, with flashes of bad memories of being used and objectified filling my consciousness.

However, my experiences are those of a white, heterosexual female. I may be oppressed based on my gender, but I recognise the privilege that I hold because of my race, my sexuality and by being a cis-gendered being. I cannot speak on behalf of all women, and I cannot understand the pain that people of colour, those within the lesbian, gay, and bisexual, transgender, queer, intersex and asexual (LGBTQIA+) community and non-gender binary individuals face.

This conscientising is another reason why the #PatriarchyMustFall movement and other discussions are so powerful: for the first time, intersectionality is not just a buzzword, but a way of understanding and navigating the world. Gender equality is really complex, as we are all individuals experiencing different manifestations of patriarchy, and so hearing about these different experiences will help everyone become passionate about the cause and understand some of these complex nuances. This is why inclusivity within this discourse is so important. By hearing the stories of women with different identities, I was given insight into the complexity, which has helped me position myself within our society.

While as a movement, we showed a great sense of camaraderie – like when we all went back into Leo Marquard to find the person who threw eggs at us while we were leaving – the complexity of gender equality means that we do not necessarily agree on everything. This is why when a man got up to speak at the mass meeting in Kopano residence, and a women expressed her disapproval and he subsequently stormed out with other men, a difference of opinion arose; some believed that we should not have silenced him, while others felt like he was intruding on the space we had created. As I sat in the front row, watching this transpire, I could not help but understand where she was coming from – as the man got up to speak, he appeared arrogant, superior and condescending. The need for her to express her contempt was valid and should not have been questioned.

This has brought into question the involvement of men in the process of dismantling patriarchy. Depending on how the space is defined, and the intention of the gathering, it is important to gauge what sensitivities are at play. While some believe that they should not have the right to comment at all – in any circumstance as they will never understand what we go through – I think men are important allies within this process and they can perform such a role if they are more cognizant of the sensitivity of this process.

There is a lot of listening that needs to take place. There is much that men do not know we experience as women, just as there is so much that I do not realise black women go through because I am white. By listening to understand, and not necessarily to respond, there is a lot of constructive learning that can take place. Furthermore, if men are able to check their privilege before they speak, and not necessarily assume they understand how we feel, it will help them to navigate the sensitivities of issues.

Discussions about patriarchy are often hard to navigate because of its multiple intersections with other issues and individual experiences based on background and teachings. This is why many people find it hard to engage with these topics. However, it is a necessity to have these discussions because they are actively changing entrenched mindsets, which are the very beliefs that have institutionalised sexism within the University of Cape Town (unequal residence rules, an underrepresentation of women in leadership, specifically women of colour, and systems that are ineffective in stopping rape and sexual abuse). As more people join in with the #PatriarchyMustFall protests, dialogues and programmes, the dismantling of these mindsets and institutions starts to take place.

I hope there will be more and more individuals experiencing that eye-opening, tear-inducing realisation that I had which will start a process for them too, of turning tears into plans and plans into change.

First published in Varsity *newspaper, 74(10): 5, 15 September 2015, http://varsitynewspaper. co.za/opinions/4259-patriarchymustfall-tears-complexities-and-realisations*

What solidarity looks likes

Sarah Mokwebo

I HAVE LEARNED, NOT ONLY through my participation and involvement in #FeesMustFall, but also through my upbringing and other social justice work, that my being as a black woman, in moments where others are not able to carry themselves, I ought to extend comradeship to others in order to continue the cause that we are collectively fighting for.

On violence and negotiation tables
Student protests have always been a highly complicated and contested space to be in as a young black person, especially as a person part of the generation that has been referred to as the 'Born Frees'. The protests are also a unique experience for women and the reasons to be part of these protests are highly personal and political to every individual.

When comrades, in historically disadvantaged universities who have constantly been wrestling with inequality in their universities, exert their frustration at the system through the use of physical force and violence, we should refuse, as those still sitting at the negotiations table on whiteness's terms in our historically white institutions, to condemn the actions of our fellow comrades. Instead, in our taking over of the narrative through the attention we are afforded by the media and society in general, it is important to highlight that violence comes in many forms, that the violence inflicted by protestors/ students is not the only form of violence taking place. These students, for more than 10 years, have exhausted all the non-violent forms of protest that white supremacy approves of in response to the injustice against them and so they find themselves in positions where they no longer have anything to lose nor to bargain with.

Different protest methods adopted at different stages of the movement often received criticism from the state and universities, but that is the purpose of protest action – to inconvenience and unsettle normalities and inspire urgency.

The cost of solidarity

Solidarity demanded from those of us, who, minutes after being shoved at the back of police vans, would have lawyers waiting for us at police stations along with bags of bail money, to hand ourselves over voluntarily in instances where fellow comrades in neighbouring universities without the resources or proximity thereof are arrested for just gathering outside the gates of universities they rightfully belong to. In our surrender, not only did we legitimise their defiance, we also fuelled the fire that needed to continue the struggle upon free bail being granted albeit with unconstitutional conditions.

As a black woman, solidarity demanded of me, after seeing another black woman being inhumanely dragged into the back of a police van along with several other male comrades, to hand myself over and be arrested along with her, because she, like myself, was already vulnerable in this world. Moreover, she would be in holding cells with many males by herself, at the mercy of a police system that has no regard for black life, in a world that does not prioritise womanhood. I feared for an eventuality that had been a reality for many women who were part of the student protests – being subjected to sexual violence.

It is unfortunate that women in the student protest movements were not safe from men whom they considered friends, brothers and comrades. In many instances women found themselves violently violated in the most horrendous ways. As feminists in the movement, we quickly came to the realisation that unity and solidarity would be the counter-force to challenge these patriarchal norms that were eating away at the soul of movement.

When a woman was sexually assaulted by another male comrade at Azania House at the University of Cape Town (UCT), patriarchy felt the need to perpetually harm and violate women by boldly demanding of women to 'dress appropriately'. Solidarity manifested through the action of all the women, queers, trans bodies in the space undressing in front of all the vile patriarchs to reiterate that our bodies belong[ed] to us and are not for the male gaze. Solidarity further called for these men to be kicked out of the space after belittling the trauma, humiliation and abuse the woman comrade experienced.

The violent nature of prisons and holding cells only recognise and acknowledge one's assigned sex and affords no regard to how one would self-identify. As a detainee, you are packed along with cis-gendered individuals, notwithstanding the offence and abuse committed towards your existence. Solidarity called for comrades, as cis-individuals, to denounce their identity and deaden the trans/non-binary hostile environment.

The explicit exclusion of queer and feminist bodies from the protest that allowed for the collective quest of liberation by patriarchal vanguards was to be countered by the refusal to partake in the protest. The refusal to partake in the exclusionary protest was a way to invalidate the exclusionary, hyper-masculine, patriarchal, partisan, pseudo revolution that continuously coddled fragile heterosexual masculinity. In solidarity, ciswomen who would be next in line to benefit from this collective effort upon the 'permission' of patriarchs, stood in solidarity and refused to form part of the protest action. Instead, a counter-protest took place.

As women, we are constantly on the opposite side of either a penis or a gun, oftentimes both. Solidarity called for the highlighting of the plight of women through symbolism when the moment called for it. The stripping off of clothes at different periods and various campuses during the student protests demanded and conveyed vulnerability which was a substantial metaphor in highlighting the war against women's bodies.

During shutdowns and occupation protests, solidarity called for one to leave their warm comfortable bed in university residence to share a thin mattress at Solomon Mahlangu House at Wits with students whom, under typical circumstances, would be homeless and not know where their next meal would come from.

We could no longer let things at South African universities remain normal. We could no longer accept that black students had to produce receipts of their poverty to access education that is promised to them in the country's constitution and the Freedom Charter. We could no longer allow gatekeepers and those commodifying education to remain comfortable in their ivory tower offices.

All this solidarity action is precisely because if you are involved in the project of creating a new future and a new world where black does not equal exploitation, then it becomes an obligation that one refuses to allow whatever privilege white supremacist heteropatriarchy capitalism affords them. One cannot absolve oneself of the responsibility of collective effort and collective liberation.

We had to demand and agitate for discomfort because that is where we found unity and where we collectively found solidarity. Solidarity, in the context of the historical moment, meant we drive instability until no single black person, child or body is subjected to the disarray of the black experience in the country on a daily basis, as is currently the case.

Your discomfort as a privileged black body is what solidarity looked like.

'I Am Stellenbosch'

Nkhensani Manabe

A GROUP OF STELLENBOSCH University students campaigning under the banner 'I Am Stellenbosch' published a controversial photo series on Facebook on 25 September 2015. In the photos, students are seen holding up white boards with various 'I am...' statements written on them. When the pictures started circulating on Twitter, they were met with disappointment, outrage, disbelief and even amusement laced with shock.

People could not understand how, in the midst of the work done by Open Stellenbosch, some students at the university were still choosing to be blind to the seriousness of transformation issues. Within days, the pictures from the campaign were shared and harshly critiqued. Supporters of the transformation project did not see statements such as 'I am white, English, and I love kwaito' and 'I am English, but I enjoy deciphering Afrikaans classes' as relevant to the cause. Such assertions highlighted the depth of the problem at the university.

Statements with the unhelpful phrase 'colour blind' or the outdated and deeply problematic racial identifier 'non-white' were made by students from all backgrounds. Clearly, many students at Stellenbosch are still ill informed and misguided when it comes to history and race relations.

The 'I Am Stellenbosch' campaign released a mission statement via its social media accounts wherein it communicated that it was a platform for understanding, recognition and acknowledgement of differences within Stellenbosch. Furthermore, its goal included being the vehicle for the advancement of university identity. It has distanced itself from other movements on campus, claiming that it isn't a response to any particular event. Despite these efforts to stand apart, it is undeniable that 'I Am Stellenbosch' could only have been possible in the wake of the unsuccessful 'Where is the Love?' campaign.

If the gist of 'Where is the Love?' was asking those who felt discriminated against 'why are you fighting with me?', then 'I Am Stellenbosch' is saying 'come on, let's all just get along!' The 'single Stellenbosch University identity', which the campaign seeks to create is not a solution to the problem of institutional racism at the university. It is a mask for those who would wilfully maintain prejudiced views to hide behind.

By purposefully redirecting the conversation at the university, the 'I Am Stellenbosch' campaign served as another silencing tactic. During a transformation project of Open Stellenbosch's magnitude, there was no time to stop and give brownie points to people who believed they were not part of the problem. Having black friends or watching *Jika Majika* (a predominantly black dance programme on SABC) does not make you exempt from the conversation about race relations on your campus.

What 'I Am Stellenbosch' showed us was how privilege and wilful ignorance could become a heady combination. It was a combination which sent people stumbling into the public space, slurring their speech while they talked about 'unity in diversity'. These people believe holding hands besides a fire whose flames are fanned by ego and empty rhetoric, while chanting 'we are a rainbow nation' will settle the score.

'I Am Stellenbosch' was what it looks like when people try to apply temporary, superficial remedies to complex problems. Thankfully, the scathing critique of this campaign indicates that those who are fighting to change the oppressive culture at Stellenbosch University will not be distracted by this tactic.

First published by Varsity *newspaper, 13 October 2015, http://varsitynewspaper.co.za/ opinions/4327-i-am-stellenbosch*

Student protests give South Africans a glimpse into hidden lives

Sisonke Msimang

JUST AS MASS PROTESTS were beginning at various campuses across South Africa, a fracas broke out among leading advocates at the country's Bar.
Leading human rights lawyer Richard Spoor was questioned about his decision to argue an important case on silicosis with an overwhelmingly white and male team. Spoor suggested he had little choice, arguing that 'we only brief exceptional counsel,' including juniors who have graduated 'summa cum laude' and 'who quite frankly border on genius'. These kinds of cases, he concluded, don't 'leave much room for charity or experimentation'.
A group of 12 black advocates – some of the country's finest lawyers – issued a public statement to Spoor, calling his comments racist. This has to date been signed by 115 lawyers. Advocate Dumisa Ntsebeza, who represented the families of miners after the 2012 Marikana massacre, suggested that the 'summa cum laude' comment was especially insulting: 'Some of us were lucky to even get to university. Some of us studied by candlelight, because there was no electricity.'
The clash between members of an elite and traditionally conservative profession offered a window into the present moment. It highlighted tensions between what renowned political scientist James C. Scott refers to as 'public' and 'hidden' transcripts. In *Domination and the Arts of Resistance: Hidden Transcripts* [Yale University Press, 1990], Scott argues that the public transcript is '...the self-

portrait of dominant elites as they would have themselves seen'. The 'hidden transcript', on the other hand, represents the voices of those who are '... off-stage, where subordinates gather outside the intimidating gaze of power'. Scott argues that when elites want to control a segment of the population they create a 'public transcript', to explain and justify their use of power in ways which often blame that group for its own oppression.

Narrative forged by colonialism

South Africa's public transcript has always been that whites are morally and intellectually superior to blacks. All the acts of domination carried out against black people, then, were justified on the basis of this core idea. The source of this narrative can be traced back to Cecil Rhodes whose 1877 confession written at Oxford included the famous words: 'I contend that we are the finest race in the world and that the more of the world we inhabit the better it is for the human race.' This became an early and – in the words of Yale University doctoral candidate Henry Trotter – 'publicly circulated' justification for colonialism. Trotter's assertion is that the statements of early colonial administrators in South Africa served as 'a screen behind which the performance of domination took place'.

It was a statue of Rhodes on the University of Cape Town's campus, incidentally, that sparked the first of 2015's student protests.

Scott reminds us that the relationship between the public and hidden is dialectical: the 'hidden' transcript is a response to the official version of events. It is a running commentary on the foolishness of those in the dominant class. So, when there is 'a rupture of the "cordon sanitaire" between the hidden and the public transcript', the results can be explosive.

It seems that we are living through precisely such a moment.

The myth of meritocracy

The apartheid-era public transcript of racial superiority has been replaced by a post-1994 discourse on merit. As the idea that white people were intellectually and morally superior to blacks fell out of favour some 20 years ago, it was substituted for a new public transcript. This insisted that whites were more meritorious than blacks. This is the idea that Spoor drew on in his ill-advised comments.

In some ways it is an archetypal myth – one that can be seen everywhere in daily life. The myth of meritocracy was called upon in countless social media posts by white South African students frustrated that their 'hard work' would be jeopardised by the actions of the protesters.

This shallow understanding of merit is the driving force behind the core disagreements between many white and black South Africans about the role and place of affirmative action in society.

In the days that followed the Spoor incident, and as the protests swelled, my social media accounts were inundated by posts from black South Africans in their 30s and 40s – my peers in the 'transition' generation – expressing their solidarity with #FeesMustFall by sharing their own accounts of surviving campus life.

There were stories from those whose parents had sold livestock to fund their transport to university and back. There were painful recollections from people who had to wait two, three, five, even seven years for their degrees because they didn't have the money to pay the registrar to release their results.

Then, as the week ended I blinked my way through the bittersweet words of a student whose family was too poor to travel to his graduation ceremony. After it was all over, he stayed seated and alone, not quite sure how he had made it. He was the last person to leave the hall.

Catharsis and hope
There was something cathartic about the stories. They had the quality of long and closely held secrets. Yet they weren't quite secrets: they were simply the kinds of invisible stories that black South Africans have been sharing with one another for generations. In every family where someone has attended university, the struggle to keep a child in school is well understood.

Among these stories of triumph and difficulty, there were many about luck and kindness and the grace of strangers. But for each story told there are countless more we will not hear. Their protagonists never made it to university because of the failure of the country's basic education system.

South Africans can no longer educate their children on the basis of luck and the goodwill of overstretched students.

The students who have been protesting since April 2015 have

not yet won the results they are after. Despite this, the mass action has served as a powerful reminder to South Africans that they are capable of far more than they are presently achieving.

Emboldened by the courage of those who took to the streets, older South Africans have also been inspired to tell their stories. We are all beginning to understand that what has been hidden must now be made public.

First published in The Conversation, *29 October 2015, https://theconversation.com/student-protests-give-south-africans-a-glimpse-into-hidden-lives-499599*

'Ignorance is the cure for nothing'

Natasha Ndlebe

'...BUT MY GUY, YOU DO know that Tshwane University of Technology [TUT] students are rejects from the University of Pretoria [UP]?' said a voice that stopped me from putting on my headphones in the minibus taxi. I turned my head around to see who had the audacity to say this, and even more so, who had the audacity to laugh so uncontrollably in agreement to this suggestion mocking my entire being. I knew immediately that this was going to be a long ride home. I listened to the two guys, who were both wearing T-shirts with the UP logo, celebrating the virtues of UP and discussing vociferously how less of a university TUT is. I listened to them arrogantly deride my intellectual inabilities and question my choices. I listened to them talk about the 'inhumane and barbaric' TUT students participating in student protests.

A few weeks earlier I had been protesting for affordable fees with my fellow comrades on campus when rubber bullets were launched onto us as though we were criminals. I was tired, my mind a blur in the heat wave, until everyone started screaming and running chaotically in all directions. This was my first participation in a strike and I was not sure what would happen after the bullets. Would 'K-9s' be released in a few minutes? Is this what post-apartheid really looked like? Was Hector Pieterson's death for nothing? All questions too big to comprehend at that moment.

And yet here I was in a minibus taxi having to listen to two benighted guys who felt the need to talk down on students and talk disparagingly about a whole university, one that has equally been fighting for correction of student inequalities with vigour and urgency. I could not believe it.

It is immensely sad that a country that fought and is still fighting for liberation and equality has ignorant young people who think the problem is students from a particular university, or women standing up and showing independence. Our problems are greater, but not close to what the youth of apartheid faced.

Being a black woman and a TUT graduate
Being a black woman tends to be regarded as irrelevant in our patriarchal society. When I refuse to accept any gender-based expectations, they call me names. When I mention that I am a TUT graduate, they dismiss me as if I made a foolish statement. So, under the circumstances one has to stand up and fight. It's not easy to keep misogynists at arm's length when women are constantly looked upon as objects. Often seen as an empty vessel made to soothe a man's ego and pride, we risk losing our lives if we dare challenge the status quo.

Patriarchy is something that even South Africa's first black woman graduate Dr Charlotte Maxeke, a committed feminist at the time, was confronted with. Maxeke founded the Bantu Women's League in 1918, the forerunner to the African National Congress Women's League (ANCWL). She met Prime Minister Botha about passes for women, which was followed by a march the following year. Considered the mother of black freedom in South Africa, Maxeke's legacy is huge and one that all women in South Africa should live to emulate. But with the current ANC Women's League and the department of women being apathetic towards the distress of women, living up to Maxeke's desires for women being able to control their destiny is hard to achieve. Fighting gender crime and inequality in this country has become equivalent to committing an unthinkable, horrendous crime.

Three years after my first encounter with a rubber bullet, I found myself within a crowd fighting for the same grievances from 2012. Fighting for basic necessities; the residences didn't have hot water almost throughout the year. TUT students were striking because of, as usual, the National Student Financial Aid Scheme. In 2012, we requested for the National Student Financial Aid Scheme to pay 30% of the students' tuition fees. We fought against the rule that made it possible for poor students to be unfairly academically excluded. The students needed another campus shuttle; just one bus travelling from Pretoria West to Soshanguve hourly was simply not enough. Even after graduating from TUT, I remained invested in student struggles and I sympathised with them.

A fight Biko would have been proud of
2015 was a remarkable year. The youth of South Africa stood together and fought, a year Steve Biko would have been proud to witness because the young people were not accepting any form of oppression from any university.

This is what made 2015 an unforgettable year, a year I was proud to witness, a historic year.

On 9 March 2015, students from University of Cape Town (UCT), longing for discussions on transformation, initiated a protest movement called #RhodesMustFall. Its initial success in the removal of Cecil Rhodes's statue ignited more student movements at other universities around the country. It became a revolutionary movement, probably the first in post-apartheid South Africa. By mid-March, Rhodes University had started the Black Students' Movement, in solidarity with the UCT's #RhodesMustFall. The movement pressed for the name of the university to be changed.

In October 2015, the University of the Witwatersrand (Wits) made an announcement that there would be a 10.5% tuition fee increment in the following year. The news caused havoc, even with other hindrances Wits students were challenging on a daily, this was the last straw. #FeesMustFall was the resulting online social media hashtag reply from the students of the university. This movement created by Wits students spread nationally and internationally to the United Kingdom in a matter of months.

In December 2017, the president announced that free subsidised education for poor and academically deserving students would be implemented. A politically driven announcement, it didn't elaborate any terms or regulations. South African students had been fighting for this for years without any success thus the announcement left some of us in limbo, craving for more clarity. But students have accepted the announcement with the hopes that it will, genuinely, be enforced because it means a black child from a rural area gets a chance and a choice.

TUT students, the misunderstood revolutionaries

After marching to the Union Buildings, I was asked to write an opinion piece based on all the hate and insults TUT students were experiencing. Initially, I was reluctant because writing in anger blinds you from being objective. 'In defence of my fellow TUT students' was nevertheless published.

The public's reaction (some of which were fellow students who were supposed to be in solidarity with us) felt like sharp wounds when they blamed TUT students for the chaos that happened at the Union Buildings without any evidence but a testimony from someone who probably wasn't even affiliated with TUT.

I found myself reflecting back to the Marikana massacre, where 34 people were killed by riot police and more than 70 others were injured. The mine workers were protesting what they believed to be exploitative labour conditions. People were killed in democratic South Africa for protesting for an end to the injustice they were facing. The police who have a responsibility to serve and protect were the ones that callously killed them. What a terrible irony.

I wrote 'In defence of my fellow TUT students' because I wanted to finally take a stand against the bullying. I wrote 'In defence of my fellow TUT students' because it is always so easy for people to be judgemental. I wrote 'In defence of my fellow TUT students' because I wanted to understand what TUT was doing wrong, when in reality they were struggling to be heard as easily and effectively as Wits, Stellenbosch and UCT students. I wrote 'In defence of my fellow TUT students' because I needed to remove the perception people have about TUT and for a minute get them to step into our shoes, understand that TUT by the mere virtue of being dominantly black, does not have the luxuries that most universities have. To so many people, TUT students are portrayed as 'stained rascals' without any morals until we stand in solidarity with the rest of the country. With that said, I don't condone violence or the reason for why buildings are burned to be heard. I condone taking a stand against a system that has shackled even our great-great grandparents from reaching their full potential.

I was totally bewildered by possibly facing the same atrocities the youth of 1976 endured in democratic South Africa. The Marikana massacre had demonstrated how easy it is for the South African police and security apparatus to revert to force equal to that used by the apartheid regime. 2015 made me understand that favouritism exists and also made me understand that I should be constantly looking for that 'envisioned self which is a free self' as Steve Biko said – 'A free self' from fighting patriarchy, fighting for transformation, free education and equality, 'a free self' that yearns for social injustices to be addressed. There is no greater pain than when a person automatically associates TUT with barbarism and with words such as 'hooligans, thugs and savages'. I recall Frantz Fanon writing in *Black Skin, White Masks* (Grove Press, 1967) that:

> In order to terminate this neurotic situation, in which I am compelled to choose an unhealthy, conflictual solution, fed on fantasies, hostile, inhuman in short, I have only one solution: to rise above the absurd drama that others have staged around me, to reject the two terms that are equally unacceptable, and through one human being, to reach out for the universal.

These words resonated with me
What is the point of trying to fight for equality if someone of the same skin colour is demeaning towards you? How do you expect this country to move forward unified?

Weeks after the publication of my article, Pontsho Pilane of Feminist Stokvel asked me to be part of a panel discussion with some amazing people driving for transformation in this country: Shaeera Kalla, Anele Nzimande and Vuyani Pambo. I am not a very vocal person, and I am still wondering how I survived that debate, but it was an honour sitting between Shaeera and Anele, the strong women who have stood up against numerous injustices, including patriarchy. Witnessing the youth-led mobilisation of thousands of students during FMF by Shaeera Kalla and Nompendulo Mkhatshwa was remarkable. Watching two women take the fight into their hands, screaming 'Amandla!' and leading many students through a revolution was something I wished I'd see more of. It is so easy for just about anyone to debate elections or debates that are not challenging enough but social justice issues, especially gender-based affairs, are ignored.

I can never thank Pontsho Pilane enough for asking me to be part of the debate because, as clichéd as this may sound, from that day I started seeing the world differently: from the questions the audience asked to being surrounded by minds that had the knowledge of our fallen heroes and craving to courageously soar their dreams into being. The same night, I got the opportunity to meet some others from the Feminist Stokvel; I might have lost the plot on meeting Lebo Mashile! The Feminist Stokvel played a big role during and after FMF protests, addressing challenges facing black women.

The Fees Must Fall and Rhodes Must Fall movements ushered in a new era which redefined youth politics in South Africa. There is so much power behind these slogans of #FeesMustFall and #RhodesMustFall. They have assisted in advancing Black Consciousness.

Conclusion

I remember reading a status message on Facebook saying, 'How do you convince upcoming generations that education is the key to success when they are surrounded by poor graduates and rich criminals?' This is where I tell young people: 'Educate yourselves, stop being ignorant.' This is where I tell that I'd rather be around poor graduates than rich criminals. We are a nation that has realised the power of mobilisation. This is where I tell them that we must look at the likes of Ida Mntwana, Albertina Sisulu, Robert Sobukwe, Anton Lembede, Bertha Gxowa etc, who refused to internalise the norms of a society that oppressed them. They refused to accept and endure any form of infractions they encountered. Therefore, young person of South Africa, question the status quo and fight for what you believe in.

Power, privilege, hypermasculinity and intersectionality

Kneo Mokgopa

2015 HAS BEEN DUBBED the year of the student because of all the protests that took place at universities. My intention in this essay is an attempt to show how protest action is gendered in the contemporary sense of the term and to propose a new model of understanding of gender which better explains the oppression of womxn, particularly in black-led uprisings like Rhodes Must Fall and Fees Must Fall.

Explaining gender and sex
Gender is in recent times becoming understood sociologically, philologically and politically as either masculine or feminine performativity. When one's sex aligns with their gender, one is considered cisgender. When one's sex does not align with one's gender, one is transgender. Transgender is a term that has gained currency with varying definitions but the one I have given will suffice for the purpose of this essay.

Black uprisings all around the world are intending to dismantle the cis-hetero-white-male-capitalist project. Most of the uprisings are taking place within university spaces or led by young people disillusioned by the postmodern assertion that all evil is behind us and that the current state of affairs is the nirvana we all need to be thankful for. In South Africa in particular, the 2015 Rhodes Must Fall campaign pulled the country's attention towards colonialism in architectural language and institutional racism. This moment in history shifted our understanding of racism to incorporate more than just bigotry but encompassed structural inequality of opportunity, historical disadvantage and systems that detect black bodies and stifle their interests to rebuke them from the institutions in which they are found.

Gender can also be seen as a layer of society that is closely related to economics and social power. This layer allocates power and privilege, using sex as a proxy. The bulk of the allocation takes place during the formative years, inducing entitlement, and forms a part of the identity. It is not the only allocator of power or privilege; race and class are others. The allocation continues in a dialectical relationship with society throughout our lives, with male bodies being offered power and privilege in various forms including the assumption of credibility. The allocation also prefers masculine performances and treats femininity as ancillary, giving them each relative power. This model sees the substance of gender as a social phenomenon and its substance is power and privilege. Bodies appealing to access power that is disenfranchised use their hypermasculinity as a defence to their ego and sense of entitlement. This model makes no inroads onto transgenderness, but rather attempts to describe and explain misogyny within black uprisings like the FMF.

Black bodies in revolt against white monopoly capitalism assert themselves as agents of power and privilege through hypermasculinity perhaps because of a failure to accept their role in oppressive social systems, seeing it as a paradox. This model does not assume that female bodies and transgender bodies have no agency for malice, it accepts this, and assumes that female and transgender bodies too access power and privilege through hyper-masculine performance.

As such, black uprisings that fail to be intersectional will often access power and privilege to disrupt white monopoly capital by accessing power through hypermasculinity, whether traditional or cultural.

The model is still vulnerable to strong rebuttal and its success and truth is yet to be tempered. In the interim, it has explained the dangers of an anti-intersectional movement as one that will be complicit in the evils it attempts to expel and further socially describes gender and sex as more relevant to each other than is currently being contested.

The Fallist activism

Rhodes Must Fall seemingly gave birth to 'Fallism', a philosophy that follows from Bantu Biko's Black Consciousness and Pan Africanism ideologues.

One Fallist comrade of mine, Athabile Nonxuba, told me that 'Fallism is an oath of allegiance to the decolonial project. It is an oppositional force against forms of domination. Fallism seeks to expel imperialism and its various forms of colonialism from Africa, which includes disturbing the hegemony of European history which has superimposed itself as an intellectual, ideological and cultural ideal in Africa. In imagining new political expressions that are able to house a collective suffering of African people despite them being from different political persuasions, Fallism to us meant an ontological and epistemological oppositional response to forms of domination.'

Fallism's ability to gather followers was evidenced in the Fees Must Fall protests across the country. However, Fallism is far from perfect. For the most part it tries to distance itself from the struggle of transgender people, and women, expressly stating that Fallism is not a feminist movement and that there is no space for the transgender agenda on the Fallist mandate, thus failing the demands of intersectionality. Further, hyper-masculine performativity is rampant in Fallist spaces. The University of the Witwatersrand attempted to extinguish hyper-masculine misogyny with the expression 'Mbokodo', leaning on the phrase 'Wa thint' umfazi wa thint' imbokodo' from yesteryear. For a moment, it seemed as though gender consciousness had finally penetrated the thick, stubborn skull of patriarchy and that Fallism would be a different form of 'umZabalazo', a modern struggle inclusive of current-day realities.

But as we know, women have been silenced for questioning the male-dominated FMF gatherings At the time of writing this essay, the university currently known as Rhodes had its naked protest after the failures of management to respond to rape and sexual violence on campus. Unfortunately, a few months after this protest a student leader took her own life protesting rape and chauvinism and the same institution.

This short essay sought to interrogate the presence of misogyny within black student movements and present a non-binary perspective. This angle is vulnerable to rebuttal, and therefore requires further enunciation.

Explained is the danger of an anti-intersectional movement as one that is complicit in the evils it attempts to expel and further socially describes gender and sex as more relevant to each other than is currently being contested.

When women become a danger to the revolution

Anele Madonsela

HOW DOES A MOVEMENT that is meant to fight against oppressive ways find itself reproducing oppressive tendencies of arrogance and patriarchal bullying? I battled with this question from the very first day to my last as one of the student leaders of the University of Johannesburg Fees Must Fall (UJ_FMF) movement.

When I tweeted challenging the University of Johannesburg (UJ) student body to join other institutions in the protests that had already gone national in October 2015, I had no idea that it would catch wind and contribute meaningfully to the national protests. UJ finally joined on 22 October 2015 under the hashtag #UJShutdown and #OccupyUJ.

As Wandile Ngcaweni would note in a newspaper article the following weekend, a handful of students including him sacrificed their sleep and braved the cold weather at 4:30 am to heed calls on Twitter to meet me at the main gate for the UJ Fees Must Fall protest, #UJShutdown. Little did we know that management had been tracking us on social media and had recruited bouncers and increased the numbers of security personnel; we did not expect to be handled and harassed by those outsourced security guards so early in the protest.

While we were tweeting about #UJShutdown, the strangest thing happened. UJ's student representative council (SRC) distanced itself from the calls for a protest and shut down. There are many reasons and stories as to why they took that decision, one being that with the upcoming SRC elections they were not prepared to boycott in order to be part of the protest. But really what was problematic was that they were a student representative body that was rejecting to be part of student mass action on campus. This decision by the UJ SRC would complicate post-protest negotiations between students and management on grievances that sparked the protests. The South African Students Congress (SASCO)-led SRC failed to capture the moment and as a result they delegitimised their claim as the voice of the student majority.

With all the successes and achievements of that monumental day, there were also many untold incidents. I attempt to recall and talk about most of the developments from the evening of the tweets to many months after I had distanced myself from the movement.

The misogynist fellow leaders

I was quite surprised to witness how things played out throughout the day that Friday of the shutdown. I suffered and had to endure sexism and misogynistic opinions from bullies throughout that time. I recall actions of individuals at the very beginning, when we marched from UJ to central Braamfontein. Comrades who were political opportunists and populists attempted to hijack the protest when it reached Braamfontein and students from the University of the Witwatersrand (Wits) joined us. It had all begun when we were marching across Empire Road. Whenever I would try to address students on plans once we reached Braamfontein, male comrades would hush me up and attempt to take over, not hesitating to remind me that I was a female not affiliated with any political party. This is when fellow student leaders from UJ and Wits told me straight to my face that I was too young to lead them and the march.

When the Wits crowd appeared, led by Nompendulo Mkhatshwa and Shaeera Kalla, I approached them to introduce myself and alert them that I was the one they had been in communication with. To my surprise, the two ladies immediately dismissed me. Shaeera simply told me that since I was not a member of the UJ SRC, they would not take me seriously. Neither would they care to hear that the UJ SRC had distanced themselves from the march. They rejected my request to march back to UJ. It was unbelievable! It was unfathomable to me that I was being bullied by fellow female comrades.

The unwarranted violence ensues

A couple of hundred Wits student comrades joined us as we marched back to UJ. Our plan was to shut down the main campus. It was time for the #UJShutDown to commence; now we had numbers, reinforcements we dearly needed for what I rightfully feared awaited us at the gates of UJ Auckland Park Campus (APK). It took us about an hour to break the line of bouncers and UJ security to gain access into campus. In the process rocks and pepper spray were used on us. On gaining access, my eyes filled with tears, I decided to go to res to change but I also felt like I needed to pray.

A few hours later, my roommate came to call me from our room. The students wanted direction as to what to do next from the leaders who called for the protests. The group had been forced out of campus and were siting and singing at the main road between Campus Square and APK. Before I could begin talking to the mass of students peacefully singing, the police arrived, asked little questions and used maximum force to disperse us all, with teargas, stunt grenades, pepper spray and even shooting at us with rubber bullets.

In the midst of these brutalities I contacted a lawyer whose legal services would prove invaluable to the movement. Tracy Lomax and some other attorneys assisted us in fighting the university when it started arresting and suspending us.

The cracks that resulted in the splits

An article by my comrade Wandile Ngcaweni in the *Sunday Independent* heightened the tensions between many individuals in the movement, especially those who had played hard at popularity politics. The article had mentioned how the UJ SRC along with many of the political organisations had refused to endorse and be part of the shutdown efforts. Slurs and insults followed, on and off social media.

Many accusations wrongfully directed at me resulted in factional splits within the movement. The SRC leadership, in their individual capacities, decided to join the movement. On several occasions, I made it clear that I had not led the UJFMF movement in order to be part of UJ's SRC. I was never interested in petty campus politics, which was why I never had loyalties of any political student organisations.

The movement quickly became tainted by toxic people who wanted to advance their political agendas in the weeks that followed. The now-energetic SRC became media frantic but did not lead or assist in any meaningful capacity. They did not concern themselves with logistics or finding sponsors for refreshments; neither did they offer to assist with communications with lawyers and legal aid matters, all of which were important in sustaining the protests.

I reached a point where bullying and attacks started to affect my physical and mental wellbeing. I could not carry the weight of #UJFMF on my own any longer and my cries for assistance always landed on deaf ears. I sacrificed a lot; my academic studies were put on hold and started to suffer. I put my mental health on the line as I forced myself to deal with the bullying, slurs and threats of 'comrades'.

At Brixton Police Station when 141 students and workers were being charged, I was at the forefront asking for assistance and physical support from students and community, while the UJ SRC chose to drink, get drunk and start causing chaos in the presence of parents and media. We would consequently spend more than 30 hours outside that police station. My tweets and those of others were able to garner more legal aid, food, blankets, refreshments etc. The UJ 141 which comprised workers, UJ students and Wits students as well as SRC leaders were all eventually released.

Personal state of mind
Those months became the most stressful and dangerous months of my life. From death threats to campus security victimisation, I had to make a decision I will hate probably for the rest of my life. I decided to leave the movement in December 2015 because the bickering from within the movement was not beneficial to the movement and I was watching it die. I did try to return to the movement as a member in 2016. I was still committed to challenging the unnatural nature of the varsity and seeing through my promise as a former leader to endure till all demands were met. Again, I failed and this time I distanced myself even further from the movement.

The many tears, my tell all
One evening we occupied our administrative building, Mafikeng, sat outside the vice chancellor's office and started studying quietly. Our intentions were pure; we just wanted to hand over our memorandum of demands personally since he was refusing to meet us or even

address us. This was when bouncers came in and threw everyone around. Men four times our size handled us with so much force that one of the students fainted and the cleaning service staff had to physically intervene in order to stop them from practically killing him with their brutality. The next day the vice chancellor told the media that students were inciting violence and disorder on his campus.

One horrific episode was when a white man from our university's campus control told me that I'm a 'kaffir bitch' for partaking in #OccupyUJ and he stated that he preferred white women because they were submissive unlike us 'kaffir bitches' that think we can lead movements. He ended off with a rant of how I would regret being a student at UJ.

I cannot help but also remember the #OccupyUJ night vigil, which was organised to peacefully pray and precisely speak out against police and campus security brutality. Police arrived as suspected because UJ management become ever more nervous of the united spirit of students. I provided them with all the permits, affidavits and all sorts of permission papers obtained for the vigil, but a few hours into the vigil the police could no longer hold their violent urges.

When rubber bullets started raining on parents, students and workers, I remember expecting to see all the speakers we had heard who claimed to be with us in the struggle mentally and physically. Shaka Sisulu was the only 'high-profile' guest and a few academic staff remained brave to protect students against the unwarranted brutality. People like Zwelinzima Vavi jumped into their German cars and quickly sped away in comfort. This kind of behaviour from high-profile leaders made us question their commitment to the movement.

The few good times
An interesting moment was during the 3rd Neville Alexander Commemorative Conference in December 2015. The conference had a huge number of non-academic staff and academics present, from whom we had felt distanced for a long time. It helped to broaden the front, bringing together staff and students on a common course of struggling for social justice.

The highlight of the #FeesMustFall movement for me though was during December 2015 when we met at the Shaft. Many Fees Must Fall representatives from many South African institutions were present. They told us their experiences; this opened my mind to other perspectives. It highlighted to me that the movement was not only difficult on me but many other students from different institutions were physically and mentally fatigued yet were positive and prepared to see the protests to the end.

Conclusion
I have written about the highs and lows that I experienced when I participated in the movement. The movement will have a permanent impact on me and I believe the protests will have a lasting impact on all students who participated in Fees Must Fall protests across South African universities. Today the state of the movement nationally saddens me – I feel the national movements of Rhodes Must Fall and Fees Must Fall failed themselves by not having common united goals. I will however be forever grateful to the lessons and experiences (good and bad) for they have made me a better person, a person who understands the moral obligations of South African citizens to seek justice at all times as well as in being agents of progress and change in society.

PART 3
WHAT FEES MUST FALL MEANS TO ME

What does a revolutionary look like?

Tshepiso Modupe

WITH MY HEAD WRAP sitting as stern as a crown, my fist in the air and a student card wrapped around my wrist, I sang as loud as my lungs could allow.

But I didn't sing, really. To say I sang sounds too pleasant.

I wailed, I roared.

I screamed into the air that I was punching, as if fighting an invisible presence. One that I had known all my life but never really understood. My mother, my grandmother and my ancestors all know of this presence. And like me, they have lived their lives fighting and finding solace in the pursuit of emancipation from it. That presence is whiteness.

In the beginning, #FeesMustFall was to me the same thing it was to any other first-year student – another of those strange university practices that senior students encourage us to be a part of. I remember it vividly. Wednesday, 14 October 2015, what one could call the launch of the #FeesMustFall campaign, was a hot, bright day, saturated with an air of expectation. We took a bus from Highfield to Main Campus and found a group of about 40 students singing under a bridge. Out of pure delight and naïvety, we pretended to know the lyrics of the songs. By the end of the first day, I had what we call at home, a 'dichubaba'* – within the course of just a day, I had an established opinion on things I could not be bothered with the day before. The ability of songs to articulate my lived experience

---

* Darkening of certain parts of the face from the excessive exposure to the sun

in ways that drive me to react, think and conceptualise still amazes me.

We did not just shut down institutions of white investment; we burned them down in each other's minds. I remember nights reading Biko and discussing Fanon in the Great Hall, feeling the immense weight of depression come over me. My comrades not only taught me but showed me what Fallist culture looks like (they could do no wrong in my eyes).

It was denim jackets, spotis,* dense literature, vast understandings of music and the poetry of black students. Their apparent pain and desolation drew me to them because I felt I could understand it, I felt their toxicities justified that I could sacrifice myself, voluntarily lose myself in the process of accommodating their brokenness. Sacrifice, I did. But accommodation remained an exhausting demand.

When I first started out, my understandings of the word 'revolutionary' existed within masculine frameworks. Leaving no space for my femininity to breathe, I would deepen my voice when speaking to a crowd or leading in song. I would shame and chastise people who did not portray the same agility in confrontation with the police or any other structure of anti-blackness. I recall now how my gait and accent transformed when it was time to agitate or mobilise.

In retrospect, not only did that limit me from feeling the state of vulnerability that I had found myself in, it limited the movement in its entirety. It was only later that cadres like Zukiswa White's would take the time to show me the importance of intersectionality as a functional, pivotal mechanism of reimagining revolutionary struggle and, furthermore, a decolonised society.

There were moments when introspective questions on my own personal politics caught my mind. The movement was male dominated, uncompromisingly hyper-masculine and strictly dismissive of feminist rhetoric.

I, feeling like I was in high school all over again, made camp with the patriarchs. I continued my stoical self-sacrifices and fully embodied the title 'patriarchal princess'. My contradictions were clear, and they were sharp. Womxn in the movement, who nurtured me and showed me a kind of love I was beginning to forget, were not only the guardians of my vulnerability, they were the same people who stood in the front of the picket lines at every shutdown and

---

* Street name for the much-popular township bucket hat

consistently spent themselves to capacity on making sure everyone remained in one piece.

These womxn, marginalised and brutalised by entitled and egotistic men, eventually began their dissent. Like a social movement within a social movement, black radical feminism took centre stage. We woke up one morning to #MBK (mbokodo) tagged all over campus and a sea of black womxn wearing multicoloured doeks and white shirts led us in song and protest during the day.

Womxn were claiming their space and it was necessary and timely. I saw this happen and I externalised myself in the fear of being accused of 'dividing the moment for your own interests', as I overheard many disgruntled men say. It was only in the moment when I endured physical sexual violence from a 'comrade' that I realised feminism to be a call to the recognition of mere existence, a call to myself to recognise that I am. And that my being is not in any way meant to be of service to any man.

The deep paralysis I felt in that moment and the days that followed turned my silent internal protests to sexism into an explicitly unapologetic performance of my feminine rage. What exacerbated my fire even more was that, at the time, I was a Wits Economic Freedom Fighters (EFF) member and the person who had violated me was also from the EFF. When information of the assault reached the centre of the organisation, absolutely nothing was said or done.

A couple of months had passed. The movement had slowed down, I had not spoken to my mother in an unhealthy amount of time and I could feel my depression deepening and darkening. From this period of my life, I do not remember a lot. I was extremely vulnerable and bewildered. I can definitely recall that my decisions were not made entirely by me.

I had a group of friends around me (with whom I would protest when the movement picked up again) and I used them as a vessel through which to live because I could not drive myself to face the realities of my emotional, physical and mental trauma from two successive years in student activism. I was numb, alone and always surrounded by people. I sought for help in various places on campus and would always be asked to fill in a form or wait until my name moved higher in the waiting list.

My situation became ironic because I was now the beautifully painful embodiment of black colour. I had deep opinions on music and literature. I made it a point to communicate black political culture through what I wore, said and sang. I was not on the outside looking in anymore; I was inside, I was as much a part of it as it was a part of me, and I hated it. I felt caged and somehow out of touch with what was real. Numerous people would exult on my spurts of anger at whites or men or buildings. I know now that my violently erratic behaviour was because I was developing a mental ailment and not necessarily because I was the most revolutionary within the pseudo-cult.

My mental disintegration reached its peak when I was in Marikana on a #FeesMustFall expedition. I was hallucinating and completely out of touch with the people I was with. Finally, my mother came to my rescue and I spent the whole of December 2016 in a psychiatric hospital. In our movement, not enough has been said or done about the mental trauma we have all undergone.

Prior to my breakdown, I had heard about comrades all over the country being admitted into hospitals and eventually forgotten. But again, black feminism and its intersectionality has had me getting monthly calls and check-ups from womxn around the country who have taught me the true image of what a revolutionary looks like. Yes, it looks like a strong mbokodo with her doek sitting as imperious as a crown, her fist in the air and the fire of her ancestors breaking down oppressive societal structures.

Revolutionary is the same woman who can allow her femininity to be her strength, guard against her vulnerabilities, courageously slashing oppressive gender privileges and allowing herself to be soft. Soft and gentle and feminine without apology.

2015, the year of the student: A personal account

Rofhiwa Maneta

Memory is an unreliable narrator. How many times have you watched your recall of a memory recede into the distance as time marches on? The details spiral out of focus and, with the absence of fact, the mind makes up its own stories. October 2015 – the month that saw the FeesMustFall movement coalesce, and ultimately, climax into a national shutdown – is now a memory that's long since receded in the rear-view of public memory.

I WAS IN A DIMLY LIT BAR in Observatory, Cape Town, on the evening before Fees Must Fall's national shutdown march. It must have been seven or eight o'clock in the evening. The blue was pulling away from the sky. A combination of blaring house music and drunken conversation was digging a hole in my ears. Plumes of cheap cigarette smoke and the smell of stale beer were dancing around the air, completing the assault on my senses.

I was exhausted!

I had spent the day following Cape Town's Fees Must Fall contingent as they marched from University of Cape Town (UCT) to Rondebosch police station to demand the release of their arrested members. Everything from the day's struggle chants to the ubiquitous 'Fees Must Fall' phrase had been looping in my head the entire day. I just wanted to unwind; insulate myself from the day's events and forget all of this was even happening.

That would turn out to be easier said than done.

Even here in this bar, with its cigarette-burned plastic table tops and toilets that refuse to flush, Fees Must Fall was very much the topic of discussion. I'd catch a bit of drunken conversation as I navigated my way across different parts of the club. 'This is unruly,' someone said. 'How is this happening,' another table chimed in. And my personal favourite, the defeatist 'but it's not like this is going to change anything'.

Protests in South Africa happen as routinely as trips to the toilet, but from the get go this felt decidedly different. A month before Fees Must Fall started, I remember sitting in Parliament listening to Stellenbosch's Vice Chancellor Wim de Villiers present his response to the Luister documentary. Even then, I remember feeling like we were on the precipice of something seismic. You could sense the students' anger as De Villiers stated that the university was 'taking transformation seriously' and that they were more inclusive than they had been in the past. He later mentioned that the university's academic staff is 71% white and that 62% of the students are white. The announcement was met with a chorus of jeers and muted laughter.

It's this kind of obliviousness that was the trip switch for the nationwide protest. Back in March, when Rhodes Must Fall began lobbying for the removal of the statue, they were at pains to state that this was about more than just the statue. Even on the day of the statue's removal, as the imposing figure of Rhodes was lifted from its tether, Rhodes Must Fall's leadership promised that this was only the beginning.

Rhodes would fall, so would patriarchy, colonisation and exorbitant university fees.

It doesn't happen very often, but there are instances when a mirror is held before our country and we see ourselves for what we truly are: broken, ugly and dancing on a precipice. Whatever disruption may have occurred during the protests is a direct response to years of financial exclusion and a higher education sector that remains only accessible to a privileged few. For the first time in our young democracy, we did away with this whole rainbow nation façade and saw ourselves for what we really are.

Later, I stumbled out of the bar.

It was just before midnight. The pavements were strewn with

drunken couples, men with cigarettes hanging from their lips and dimming streetlights. I didn't know it at the time, but during the next few weeks, history would unfold in front of my eyes. The students would successfully negotiate a zero-percent fee increase, end outsourcing in some universities and march to Pretoria's Union Buildings. In those few weeks, the idea that young South Africans are apathetic was smashed to pieces but also, on a personal level, I felt hopeful.

If October 2015 proved only one thing, it's that the kids are alright.

I did not think Rhodes would ever fall, but he did. Fees also fell in December 2017, although there is much detail that still needs to be ironed out in order to celebrate it as a genuine victory that will benefit all students. The announcement by government on fee-free higher education for poor students is the beginning of something that will certainly be a corrective measure to confront intergenerational poverty. If we have learned something from South Africa's history, it is that there are no complete victories; revolutions such as #FeesMustFall are continuous and have no expiry dates.

This article first appeared on Live Magazine SA on 18 December 2015. Available at: http://livemag.co.za/vip/2015-the-year-of-the-student/

Convocation speech at Stellenbosch University – Courage, compassion and complexity: Reflections on the new Matieland and South Africa

Lovelyn Nwadeyi

MOST SOUTH AFRICANS are raised to refer to someone older than them with some sort of a prefix. In Xhosa, you would usually refer to an older woman as 'uMama' and an older man as 'uTata'. 'USisi' and 'uBhuti' would be used to address a younger woman and a younger man. These words respectively would mean 'mother, father, sister and brother'. With my English friends, I always referred to their moms and dads as 'Aunty So and So' and 'Uncle So and So' if we had a close relationship. In the event that I wasn't as informal with their parents I would call them 'Mrs and Mr So and So'.

When I started learning Afrikaans, I was taught that someone older than you or not related to you was then referred to as 'Meneer' (in the case of a man) and 'Oom' could be used in the event that you had a less formal relationship with the person in question. The terms 'Mevrou' and 'Mejuffrou' correspond as the English equivalents of 'Mrs' and 'Miss' that we use for women and again for less formal relationships one could refer to an older woman as 'Tannie'. What you never did in Afrikaans, however, was to use the term 'jy' (the informal term that corresponds to 'you' in English) for an elder, a stranger or your parents. Using 'jy' in Afrikaans for an elderly person or someone who you didn't quite well know was considered disrespectful. 'Jy' was only used among equals, among friends, family and colleagues that had a special understanding with each other. 'U' was the adequate term – to indicate respect mostly used in formal settings and when referring to God; otherwise the proper terms of 'Mamma', 'Pappa', 'Mevrou' and 'Meneer' would suffice.

And so, you can imagine the predicament that I found myself in when I started to visit the homes of some of my friends from school and even at university. The setup was as follows: the domestic worker in the house would be old enough to be my mother or even my grandmother. I would walk into the house and greet her with a 'Molo Mama' (because that was how I was raised) and my friend would greet her with a 'Hello Florence/Priscilla/Cynthia' (on first name basis it seemed they were). In requests for said domestic worker to bring something or make lunch, it was always the pronoun 'jy'. It became awkward for me to see someone who looked like me and was three or four times my senior not being referred to with the same respect that my friends and their families would otherwise have afforded another individual of that age group if they were not a maid and if they were not a person of colour. It began to dawn on me that I was taught to speak a language foreign to me with respect for its speakers, but that respect was not to be extended to people that looked like me. We could only ever be 'jy'.

And so you see, members of this convocation, that although this is a small example, it is in such ways that we are able to subtly use language to exercise power over other people. Dat ons nie vir ander mense die respek gee wat ons eie taal vir ons leer om te doen nie, wys vir my dat waar ons die geleentheid het, sal ons taal gebruik om mag oor ander mense uit te oefen.

Dames en Here, Lede van die US Konvokasie, goeienaand.

Toe ek verlede jaar die uitnodiging ontvang het om 'n toespraak te lewer, was ek redelik onseker oor wat ek moet sê. Die waarheid is die Stellenbos van 2010–2012 is baie anders as vandag se Stellenbos. Dit voel vir my dat so baie het verander maar ook dat so baie het dieselfde gebly... And so for this reason, I have decided to keep this address within the bounds of honest reflection, painful truths and hopeful outlook.

I do not take for granted the fact that I am the first woman, the first black person and the youngest person to address some of the most powerful white people in South Africa at this convocation today.

When I look back on 2015 and the last 26 days of 2016, I am reminded again that it has been an incredible time in South Africa in which our social consciousness has been stretched, awakened, challenged and perhaps even tampered with. Who amonsgt us here would have thought that while we were making our resolutions in January 2015 that somehow Rhodes would been given the time-out signal at the University of Cape Town? Who among us saw it coming that Stellenbosch would be subpoenaed by its very own students, demanding that the ancient doors of education here truly be made open to all South African citizens? Which of us can say that we foresaw the eruptions of unapologetic Black Consciousness at what is currently known as Rhodes University and Wits university while we were planning to start banting and lose 20 kilos last year? Did any of us think that we would all serve as witnesses to Emmanuel Sithole's brutal murder, the Mozambican man, whose only crime was perhaps to have lost in the lottery that is citizenship and make his way over the border into an unwelcoming Johannesburg? How could we have known that in supposed attempts to manage the situation, some members of our police force would laugh and giggle while foreigners sizzled in rubber rings on the streets of Durban? I'm quite sure that none of us saw #FeesMustFall coming, or the macabre images of students being shot at and teargased at Parliament, the supposed home of our democracy.

Indeed, almost 22 years into democracy, in the 60th year since the Freedom Charter's adoption and just six months before the 40th year anniversary of the June 16 uprisings, South Africans are now faced with the task of looking into the mirror and asking themselves: 'What is this that is happening all around us?' and 'Why does it feel as it does?' The problem, however, is that there are perhaps 60 million different versions of this question being asked, in more than 11 languages. It may seem as though only some of these voices are being heard, but it is becoming clear that the rainbow nation ideal promised in 1994 is becoming an ever-distant one. Perhaps we are starting to realise that there was no rainbow to begin with.

Ladies and gentlemen, something is brewing in South Africa. I do not know the name of that something, but I know that it is irreversible and will continue to brew and boil over whether we give it permission to do so or not. Without sounding like a prophet of doom, I bring your attention to my speech, as it stands in the programme. It is entitled Courage, compassion and complexity: Reflections on the new Matieland and South Africa.

Tonight however, it is difficult for me to talk courage or compassion. I am painfully reflecting on the new Stellenbosch and the new South Africa; I am cautiously and ashamedly questioning what is significantly new about both establishments. I have struggled through a number of personal conflicts over the last year and I can only speak from the point of the thought processes I am undergoing as a South African youth.

I will firstly say that we owe it to ourselves as South Africans to be honest and vulnerable with each other. In her October 2015 article entitled 'Conservative backlash comes from unexpected quarters', Sisonke Msimang writes the following:

> There should be nothing we cannot discuss in a democracy that so many people died to produce. Indeed, the primary contribution of this new generation of activists to the future must involve raucous debates about the Constitution and the utility of some of its clauses in a still unequal society. Instead of adopting a sneering tone, those who fought for freedom ought to be grateful that 'post-apartheid' citizens are insisting on honest racial dialogue. Those who claim to be committed to democracy must be pleased that new voices are questioning the faulty economic approaches the country has taken thus far.

In the wake of the ugly racial, political and economic debates happening in South Africa, I can tell you as a young person that there is a new generation of South Africans, especially those of colour, who are proud and have no interest or tolerance for the things their parents let slide as we entered the democratic dispensation. In essence, this means that as we define and redefine our identities, and as we define the new South Africa that we want our identities to manifest in, we have created no room for capitalists without conscience, no room for racists, patriarchs, misogynists, homophobes, 'ageists' or 'ableists'. The inappropriately labelled 'born frees' are saying that we will employ an intersectional feminism that squarely confronts the systems of oppression that neither the TRC nor the current South African Constitution has been able to sufficiently address. The kinds of young South Africans I have encountered in the last while are unapologetic and no longer interested in molly-coddling fragile egos or 'catching feelings'.

What our schools and universities refused to teach us and include in our curriculums we have gone out and taught ourselves. This means that in our conceptualisation of the new and the old, in our understanding that our ancestors were not savages, that they did in fact write their own philosophies about life and society, and that our fathers and forefathers did in fact have a religion of love and justice and mercy captured in the holiest and purest form of 'Ubuntu' before the Europeans arrived with Bibles in one hand and guns in the other hand, in our understanding that our ancestors were not only good enough for slavery, we are becoming clearer in our intent that that which came with the old system must be dismantled in order to truly say we are living in or at least building towards a more equitable and humane society.

The real issue is that in this democratic moment in South Africa, each of us with our diverse interests, agendas and privileges has a very clear decision to make. Do we want to be part of a new South Africa? Do we even think that Stellenbosch is part of South Africa? Because in as much as we want to insulate ourselves in this little Europe, we must be very clear that Stellenbosch is not exempt from the winds of change that are blowing through the country. Stellenbosch is in fact part of the Republic of South Africa and is largely responsible for many of the inequalities in it today. Sometimes I think that when we talk about our institution, we forget that the actual academic thesis for apartheid was casually written in black and white just down the road in the sociology department of this university.

Today I am standing in the DF Malan Sentrum where I graduated with beautiful results in 2012, and when I walked across this stage, I had never been so happy to have a white man tap me on the head. But the reality is DF Malan, the man after whom this building was named, would have never wanted me here. To DF Malan, I was only good enough to be a slave, yet here I stand with a master's in Peace and Conflict Studies cum laude. When the Verwoerd plaque in Dagbreek came down last year, I couldn't believe the outrage some people expressed at its removal as though there was any good to his thoughts about humanity?

The truth is that white South Africans will never understand what the experience of racism really means. It's not just about being called a monkey by a Sparrow. It's not just about being told you are a 'messed-up race that opens its legs just to get a child-grant' as Marie van Rensburg brazenly claimed a few days ago; it is a daily psychological violence that manifests in every single area of one's life. It infiltrates religion and one's perception of self, it infiltrates the economy, it infiltrates politics and it infiltrates education. White people will never understand what it is like to be taught a false history of your own people but not in your language and yet in a building named after a man who thought you were intellectually and scientifically inferior to his own.

To be studying at a school or have a degree from an institution literally built on the labour, the suffering and the land of your own people, and then be confronted with that every single day is a distasteful experience. This is not something that we were simply supposed to get over after 1994.

The reality is that a system that was racist, patriarchal and unconscionable in its capitalism on Tuesday, 26 April 1994 did not magically change on Thursday, 28 April 1994. And this is why we are still having the same conversations. A recent tweet from Khaya Dlanga captured this perfectly.

While I deeply respect and honour the legacy of Nelson Mandela, one of the greatest mistakes I believe he and his comrades made was to tell their people to 'forgive before an apology was offered'. In South Africa, contrary to other normal peace processes, 'forgiveness was given before the crime was acknowledged by the perpetrators'. The TRC was supposed to deal with our issues of forgiveness and reconciliation, but the evidence of the last few months is to the contrary and people are not interested in having their anger policed or curated.

The problem, I think, in South Africa is that we are not all 100% convinced that our past was unjust. The Germans are genuinely sorry (barring the right-wing neo-Nazis); as a country, Germany is so embarrassed by their history that Nazism and public glorifications of Adolf Hitler are criminalised. There is no in-between that some aspects of Nazi Germany were good or some parts of it were bad. Germans have outright written that part of their history off as unequivocally bad. In South Africa, there is no consensus that ±400 years of colonialism and 52 years of apartheid was an affirmative action for white people at its best. Today we still debate the legacy of

Rhodes and not all of us agree that our history was in no way pretty by any measure because you still hear people talking about 'die goeie ou dae...'

Ons land is in groot moeilikheid en Stellenbos is in groot moeilikheid, maar nie as gevolg van die tradisionele 'swaart gevaar' nie of as gevolg van 'die kanker van Engels nie'. Ons is in die moeilikheid want ons het komplekse probleme wat ons moet aanspreek en dit benodig 'n heel ander vlak van moedigheid en dapperheid om die spoke van ons lelike geskiedenis aan te spreek.

I realise that at the moment many of my white friends are struggling to find and even articulate what their place and role in the new South Africa is or should be. And I realise for sure that our government has not been faithful to its commitments after 1994. We definitely have a crisis of leadership and good governance in South Africa, and it will take a concerted effort by individual South Africans to hold our politicians accountable.

However, nothing that we are experiencing and feeling is happening in isolation from what we see manifesting on a national level.

We as a nation are the sum total of our experiences.

We are a mess and we must acknowledge that mess. We cannot attempt to erase that from our social consciousness. When we choose not to listen and extend practical compassion to the most marginalised amongst us, we do our own narrative as a nation a great disservice.

Without compassion, in this country we will not survive the current tumultuous times we are in.

Practically, this means that 2016 is the year that white South Africans must listen and take the back seat in conversations about race, power and privilege. Black South Africans had to give forgiveness in 1994 simply to get a vote. In 2016 if black South Africans are to continue giving with that mantra, it must be reciprocated with compassion and active forms of retribution. No matter what our individual sentiments, South African women of colour got the shortest end of the stick in the negotiated settlement and it is evident that their children are coming back for a refund...

Soos ek voor hierdie Konvokasie staan, besef ek dat daar is mense wat sal voel ek is anti-wit, ek is rassisties en dat ek meld myself aan asof ek al die antwoorde het vir Suid-Afrika se probleme. Maar ek wil graag hê dat u sal mooi luister vir dit wat ek sê. Vir dié van ons wat vas glo dat my gedagtes en perspektiewe is 'n aanval teen Afrikaans en teen wit Suid-Afrikaners, wil ek dit baie duidelik maak dat ek het geen belangstelling om teen enige ras-groep of taal-groep te staan nie.

Wat ek wel glo is dat ons moet altyd eerlik met mekaar wees in sulke gesprekke oor ons land, ons universiteite en die toekoms waarheen ons gaan. Die 'koei in die bos', wat ek glo Prof Breytenbach nog gaan aanspreek is hierdie kwessie van taal. Die ding met taal en hoe ons dit gebruik is dat dit is nooit neutraal nie. Veral in die konteks van Suid-Afrika en Stellenbos – taal is net so persoonlik soos wat dit polities is.

Vir my is dit baie belangrik om te erken dat die US 'n Suid-Afrikaanse universiteit is. Die behoort aan alle Suid-Afrikaners en nie aan een groep nie. To be part of this country, the underlying thesis that we have all implicitly accepted is that South Africa belongs to all who live in it. And unless we want to have another CODESA we cannot now start to delineate and decide who gets to study where on the basis of language.

Tweedens wil ek vinnig praat oor hierdie kwessie van die beskerming van 'n taal. Soos u kan hoor, praat ek baie mooi Afrikaans. Ek is nie 'n Afrikaner nie en ek het nie Afrikaans op Stellenbos geleer nie, maar ek is baie lief vir die taal. Vir my is daar woorde en gevoelens wat ek nie beter kan beskryf in 'n ander taal nie. Maar, ek dink die primêre funksie van 'n universiteit is nie noodwendig om 'n taal of 'n kultuur te beskerm nie maar om hoër onderwys te voorsien vir die dogters en seuns van ons land. Waar hierdie toegang tot opvoeding vir alle Suid-Afrikaner studente beperk word d.m.v. taal moet ons dan herevalueer of die universiteit eintlik sy werk doen of nie.

Afrikaans gaan nie sommer sterf nie as dit nie meer die hoof taal van onderrig is nie. Vra net vir ander mense wat nogsteeds hulle taal praat sonder 'n universiteit.

Laastens wil ek praat oor die taal self. Die groot vraag hier is 'Aan wie behoort Afrikaans?' Die eenvoudige antwoord is dat dit behoort aan Afrikaners.

But who owns Afrikaans?

The Kaapse Klopse with their Ghoema Musiek should rightfully own Afrikaans. The people of District Six and the Bo-Kaap should rightfully own Afrikaans. The face of Afrikaans at Stellenbosch University should not only be the face of a white man, but also the face of coloured Afrikaans women and black Afrikaans women too. Because they do exist no matter how much we deny them access to our university. We must stop this thing of using coloured and black Afrikaans people who are currently dispossessed as our farmworkers and cleaners as an excuse for exclusionary policies and practices. The very act is exploitative in nature because we know that their children will never make it to Stellenbosch University as it is. But even if their children do make it to Stellenbosch, they will arrive here and see an Afrikaans language and culture that is foreign to them; defended in their name yet one in which they have no part.

Die groter waarheid is dat Afrikaans is baie tale, dit is baie verskillende kulture. Ons moet erken, dat Afrikaans is in ons eie geskiedenis (en selfs vandag) baie keer gebruik teen mense wat nie wit is nie. As ons vir 'n Afrikaanse-universiteit wil verdedig, dan moet ons aanvaar dat dit behels onder andere 'n verdediging van: Afrikaaps, Swartlands Afrikaans, Bolands Afrikaans, Overbergs Afrikaans, Weskus-Sandvelds Afrikaans, Karoo-Afrikaans, OosKaaps Afrikaans, Oranjerivier- en Gariep-Afrikaans, Boesmanslands, Griekwa-Afrikaans, Namakwalands en Richterveld-Afrikaans. En dan moet ons erken dat die gesig daarvan is meestal nie die gesig van 'n wit Afrikaner man nie. Ons moet erken dat baie min mense is verbind tot die beskerming van alle vorme en alle gesigte van Afrikaans in die nuwe Suid-Afrika.

Ons moet erken en herken dat die ontwikkeling en onderhoud van Afrikaans as 'n akademiese taal, as 'n kultuur en as 'n magtige ekonomiese en sosiale gereedskap was nooit bedoel of bestem om 'n nie-wit bevolking te beskerm nie. Dus kan die teenwoordigheid van 'n Afrikaans-sprekende Kleurling populasie nie gebruik word as 'n rede om US te behou soos wat dit nou is nie net omdat dit gemaklik is in hierdie gesprek. Dit wys dat ons net belangstelling in kleurling studente en mense het wanneer dit die doeleindes van 'n wit Afrikaanse agenda pas en dit is baie oneerlik.

On this note I want to end my speech by saying that we have a choice as South Africans to reclaim our humanity. Both apartheid and colonisation dehumanised us all by giving white people a superiority complex and giving black people an inferiority complex (albeit with different consequences). We must dismantle this inhumanity that we are all products of by reclaiming our collective humanity. We must reclaim our histories so that our children grow up knowing the truth about themselves. We must reclaim our languages so that those who choose to learn and speak them do so out of pure love for our languages and not out of obligation.

I look forward to the day when I do not have to talk to my children about racism or sexism. That is really my dream for South Africa and Africa as a whole. But to get to this point, we have to have some difficult conversations. When these conversations happen, we must know the roles we are to play. Those who must listen must listen, those who need the chance to cry must cry. Those who need to be angry must be angry. Those who need to talk must talk. But none of us gets to claim an easy victory. Because there is no victory in our collective pain, there is only closure. And South Africa desperately needs closure.

Convocation speech delivered at Stellenbosch University, 27 January 2016

Black thoughts on white psychology: A student's perspective on curriculum transformation

Kgaugelo Sebidi

Introduction

THE RHODES MUST FALL (RMF) movement has undoubtedly compelled many in the South African academy to re-examine, rethink and reconsider the status quo of education in the country. RMF began as a protest against the prominent statue of well-known colonialist, Cecil John Rhodes at the University of Cape Town (UCT) in 2015 and it catapulted into a movement which questioned the pervasive institutional culture of the university as it appeared to favour 'white bodies' at the expense of blacks. I was a postgraduate student at UCT when all this prevailed, and admittedly, what began when Chumani Maxwele threw faeces at a statue, has left a lasting impression on my academic life. The RMF movement has inspired to me revisit and critically engage with my academic experiences of being a psychology student at the University of Johannesburg (UJ) from 2012 to 2014.

This paper is therefore an autoethnographic account of my time as a student at UJ. Although written in hindsight, it offers valuable insights of my pedagogical experience of the field. As most autoethnographies often interweave the personal to broader debates, I also attempt to analyse how the pedagogics of psychology translate in its practise in South African society, particularly when it comes to mental health. As previously noted, this paper utilises auto-ethnographical writing as a research method.

According to Neville-Jan, (2003: 89) 'Auto-ethnography is an alternative method and form of writing falling somewhere between anthropology and literary studies'. This kind of method is a no-holds-barred approach to writing, and it utilises personal experiences in substantiating for postulations. Nonetheless, it is not meant to be self indulgent or narcissistic, but it aims to relate the self to other phenomena outside the self. As Denshire (2013: 2) articulates, 'While auto-ethnography contains elements of autobiography, it goes beyond the writing of selves. Writing that crosses personal and professional life spaces goes further than autobiography whenever writers critique the depersonalising tendencies that can come into play in social and cultural spaces that have asymmetrical relations of power.' In this paper, I use this research method deliberately as most traditional scientific approaches still often require researchers to 'minimize their selves, viewing self as a contaminant and attempting to transcend and deny it' (Wall, 2006: 1).

The discovery of passion
I was raised in a working-class township and attended a local primary school in Daveyton in the East Rand region of Johannesburg. After grade 7, my mother thought it would be wise to send me to Burgersfort, a rural part of Limpopo to live with my grandmother. Although living in the village was difficult in various respects, it espoused moral character and resilience within me.

After completing high school, I could not pursue further studies as I had not applied to university. Life in rural Limpopo tended to be insular, and to be honest, only a few in my grade 12 class even knew first-hand what a university looked like at the time. After high school, I went back to Daveyton to live with my mother and I tried to figure out the next move for my future. I always aspired to become a medical doctor but the 44% maths mark that I obtained in grade 12 (due to a lack of a teacher) meant that I was disqualified before I could even apply for a medical degree.

Coming back to the township had its advantages; I started frequenting the local Jerry Moloi Library which was less than 3 kilometres from my home. It was in this library where I first picked up a psychology textbook. The book was part of a seven-volume series on psychology. These were reference books and I could only read them in the library. The first volume was about the history of psychology, the second was about the brain and the nervous system and the third was about psychological theories.

The books had a chronological order which eased one's immersion into the subject. By the time I read the sixth volume I was enamoured by psychology. A friend of my mine once jokingly quipped that I was the kasi (township) psychologist as I would recite Dr Phil's* lines when trying to 'counsel' my friends. I applied for a BA psychology degree at the University of Johannesburg and got accepted with government funding.

In 2012, I began my studies at the university, and fell more in love with the field. I remember on our first day of orientation, a psychology lecturer welcomed us in the Sanlam Auditorium and gave his speech. As he concluded, he quoted Viktor Frankl. I was so excited that he quoted an author I knew. I hurriedly tried to explain that Frankl was a psychiatrist and holocaust survivor to another first-year student sitting next to me, but I doubt he paid me any attention.

The academic experience

The three years studying psychology as a student at UJ were the most incredible years of my life. I understood the content, got along with the lecturers and even worked for the psychology department for the last two years of my degree. I wanted to be a psychologist and everyone around me thought I would make a good one.

But to their disappointment, I left psychology for development studies, as the interest in my first love had waned in my third year of study. As a senior student, I was now aware of various pertinent issues which continued to affect my country. I felt that psychology equipped me with the tools of understanding the individual (micro) but now I was ready to tackle societal issues (the macro). My move away from psychology can be attributed to a number of reasons but my experience of being taught the discipline contributed to my eventual decision to pursue a different field.

While psychology owes its scientific genealogies to Europe and America (Meuller, 1979), its contemporary manifestations ought to reflect existing diverse global demographics – both in pedagogy and in curriculum. However, in post-apartheid South Africa, psychology

---

* Dr Phillip McGraw, host of the American talk show *Dr Phil*.

remains a subject of critique due to its lack of transformation in the learning environment. This, of course, is not new as Sehlapelo and Terre Blanche (1996) once noted that psychology was at historical crossroads after South Africa became a democratic country. Chabani Manganyi (1973) also noted much earlier the challenges of relevance facing psychology in South Africa, particularly in practise.

In my first year, we used an American textbook called *Psychology: The Science of Mind and Behaviour* by Passer and Smith (2008). The book provided us with the basics of psychology but it was based on a North American setting throughout. In second year, this trend would continue as we were still reading North American textbooks for topics such as developmental psychology, social psychology, positive psychology and personality psychology. In third year, we were taught research methods in psychology, cognitive psychology and psychotherapy – all with the aid of American textbooks. The only exception was psychopathology for which we had a South African textbook, but it was still heavy with data and information from America.

But being taught all this content for three years without a single black lecturer was disheartening. I remember while in a class for cognitive psychology, our lecturer tried to demonstrate how biases and stereotypes are wired in the brain. He said, 'Imagine you are driving, and you see a female driver make a mistake on the road – that could lead you to believe that all women can't drive.' Although this example had merit in terms of describing biases and stereotypes, it was laden with an assumption that all students in the predominantly black class could drive or have access to a car, thus revealing a possible socio-economic class dynamic which could have been distorted. Perhaps saying 'Imagine you're in a bus or taxi' could have been a better use of words.

At the time, it was hard to notice any contradictions within the curriculum, the examples used or even the lecturers. Added to that, psychology was taught in an apolitical manner and we all assumed that it related to everyone. But in the process, it silently dehumanised some of us. This experience is reminiscent of Freire's (1970: 71) notion of the 'banking concept of education as an instrument of oppression' where the teacher's role is 'to "fill" the students of his narration contents which are disconnected from reality, disconnected from the totality that engendered them and could give them significance'

(Freire, 1970: 71).

To express this in a less politically correct way, to encounter psychology was to encounter whiteness. A state of being which I unconsciously always aspired towards, hence it was hard to question. I thought psychology was going to sprinkle me with a few white flakes which would help me manoeuvre the academic ladder through educational advancements – but instead, the whiteness was showered upon me. I was immersed into a world which was not my own. Everything I was taught distanced me from who I was and my constituency.

It was fascinating to read about Euro/American psychology, however, it truly detached one from their immediate reality and took them to a parallel universe. Education is an important aspect of identity formation (Luckett, 2012). Even Msila (2007: 47) argues that 'education is not a neutral act in that it both draws on existent student identities and attempts to construct certain identities in learners'. And through this academic experience, I was indeed forming a new identity, an identity different from my original one. To borrow from W.E.B. Du Bois (1903), this was my own double-consciousness. This can also be expressed through the coloniality of knowledge and being – the former speaks to the epistemological colonisation and the displacement of alternative knowledge's (Nontyatyambo and Ndlovu-Gatsheni, 2013), while the latter speaks to the 'othering' of those previously colonised and the questioning of their humanity (Maldonado-Torres, 2007).

The reckoning of change

I am pleased that the department of psychology at UJ has taken some of the matters discussed in this essay seriously, although this was after I had left the university. I visited the department in the last quarter of 2017 and met its new head of the department, who was the first ever person of colour to occupy the position and mentioned the strides that the department has made since I left. The department now has 57% of academic staff from designated groups, compared to 30% in 2013, and it hosted its inaugural Psychology and Decolonisation Colloquium in 2017. The head noted that there were many challenges, but the department was implementing change, particularly in curriculum and staff demographics. It is therefore my hope that future undergraduate students will be taught to be more critical of psychology and how it relates to the South African context.

Conclusion

In conclusion, it appears that psychology and mental health in South Africa are at critical junctures. While the debates about how to transform or decolonise the discipline ensue, there are some changes that can begin in the lecture hall and this may have a spill-over effect to mental health in general. My experience of being taught psychology was apolitical and it lacked contextual, social and cultural relevance. As psychology is mostly about the individual, it becomes easy for students to see parts of themselves within it. However, to depoliticise the discipline in a country which experienced colonialism and apartheid will not help, especially because the legacies of past regimes continue to exist in less obvious forms. The pedagogical experience of psychology needs to be inclusive. Not in a 'black nationalistic' (Jansen, 2017: 34) way, but in a way which appreciates diversity and the relevance challenges that plague the field.

References

Denshire, S. 2013. 'Autoethnography', *Sociopedia.isa*: 2.

Freire, P. 1970. *Pedagogy of the Oppressed*. Continuum: New York.

Health Professions Council of South Africa. 2017. 'Statistics'. Available at: http://www.hpcsa.co.za/Publications/Statistics. Accessed on 1 October 2018.

Kessi. S. 2017. 'Decolonising psychology creates possibilities for social change', *The Conversation*. Available at: https://theconversation.com/decolonising-psychology-creates-possibilities-for-social-change-65902. Accessed on 1 October 2018.

Luckett, K. 2012. 'Working with "necessary contradictions": A social realist meta-analysis of an academic development programme review', *Higher Education Research and Development*, 31(3): 339–52.

Maldonado-Torres, N. 2007. 'On the coloniality of being: Contributions to the development of a concept', *Cultural Studies* 2(3): 240–70.

Manganyi, C. 1973. *Being-Black-in-the-World*. Ravan Press: South Africa.

Msila, V. 2007. 'From apartheid education to the revised national curriculum statement: Pedagogy for identity formation and nation building in South Africa', *Nordic Journal of African Studies*, Vol. 16(2):146–160.

Nontyatyambo, P. D. & Ndlovu-Gatsheni, S. J. 2013. 'Power, knowledge and being: Decolonial combative discourse as a survival kit for pan-Africanists in the 21st century', *Alternation* 20(1): pp.105–34.

Neville-Jan A. 2003. 'Encounters in a world of pain: An auto ethnography', *American Journal of Occupational Therapy*, 57(1): 88–98.

Passer, M. & Smith, R. 2008. *Psychology: The Science of Mind and Behaviour*. McGraw Hill: Boston.

Sehlapelo. M. & Terre Blanche, M. 1996. 'Psychometric testing in South Africa: Views from above and below', *Psychology in Society* 21(1): 49–59.

Wall, S. 2006. 'An auto ethnography on learning about auto ethnography', *International Journal of Qualitative Methods*, 5(2): 1–11. Available at: https://sites.ualberta.ca/~iiqm/backissues/5_2/PDF/wall.pdf. Accessed on 1 October 2018.

Sentimentality in remembrance or The born are not yet free

Enhle Lucinda Khumalo

IF IT IS INDEED TRUE that every day is a different day,
Then tomorrow is Another Country,
Where centuries happen in a week.
But we must have been nostalgic,
Singing the Song of Solomon,
Because lately, on every other day
The same day keeps happening.
Biko,
We are still as Black as Sunlight,
And as rich as the House of Hunger.

Many South Africans support #FeesMustFall: An open letter to David Maimela

Busani Ngcaweni

Dear Comrade Dave,

Thank you for provocatively extracting an opinion from me on this matter of #FeesMustFall. As you may know, due to my position in government I always avoid commenting on issues where a conflict of interest might arise. Of course, my seniors always rationalise things a lot, so they always distinguish between the pedestrian opinions contained herein and expositions that might bring the state into disrepute.

But more pointedly, you want to know why senior people in the ruling party are supportive of the Fees Must Fall movement when they preside over the resources and state power yet lament the state of affairs as if they are in the opposition benches like #AskMmusi (remember that social media gimmick by the leader of the opposition), who was chased away by protesting students this week.

Well, my friend, I am not a spokesperson, so I can't give you the official line. But I have an inkling of why there is popular support for #FeesMustFall. Let me give this a shot, without sounding like a social development official ranting about social grants or a taxi operator who screams 'these taxi people can't drive'. I know this oxymoron might not immediately make sense. That is the point; we tend to lose each other in our own language.

The first problem is the manner in which students are being treated by university authorities, who are very patronising. They regard students as children and very often bully them and treat them in a condescending manner. They also say negative things about the student leadership.

If you ever fail a course, they leak your records so the world starts to doubt you. But this is not new. People like Professor Paulus Zulu of the University of KwaZulu-Natal used to play those dirty games and even plant stories in the newspapers about the academic performance of student leaders.

Many vice chancellors like the University of the Free State's Jonathan Jansen have said on record that student leaders are uncultured, with no creativity and value for education. Yet, they preside over billions of rands worth of intellectual capital which they can draw on to enrol the student in various strategic leadership courses such as the art of negotiations, diversity, political theory, international relations, etc.

But that is not the point. It is not about the students' (in)ability to bargain during fee negotiations or them making politically divisive statements. For authorities, the issue is ideology and the craft is the exercise of power. If students don't buy into what the authorities are selling, they are often labelled all manner of pejoratives. I once put it to Professor Adam Habib of the University of the Witwatersrand (Wits) that instead of expelling Mcebo Dlamini, maybe Wits should have mobilised its internal intellectual resources to get Mcebo to learn and appreciate history and international relations, thus building a proper understanding of why there is no room for progressive people to celebrate any inch of Nazi Germany.

Many people observe this disdainful attitude towards the students and sympathise. I for one am fully behind them. We were treated the same way as student leaders in the late 1990s. Also as a parent, I think it shows a lack of insight to close down campuses each time there is an agitation. There are civilised ways of stabilising the situation rather than putting students out on the streets where they become vulnerable to all manner of situations due to their socio-economic conditions. This is what homeland and apartheid administrators used to do. Just check how easy it is for the Tshwane University of Technology to issue ultimatums about removing poor students from campus.

Many people also find it odd that these institutions have senior leaders who offer opinions about matters of governance in the state (as they are fully entitled to do) yet they can't apply some of their recommendations to the situations in their institutions. They talk about accountability, creativity, transparency and transformation, yet the principles are not extended locally. As I have said before, due to my position in government, there are ethical bounds (not necessarily legal) to what I can and cannot say.

I suspect many people see these varsity administrators commenting on many national issues and ask themselves: Why can't they use all their capital to address students' and workers' concerns in their own institutions? I am attracted by this question. How can the holders of intellectual capital behave the same way as some small corner café which struggles to deal with a fluke cook who eats most of the cheese rather than serve it to customers? Many academics who occupy the public discourse space bemoan poor stakeholder consultation and communication from the state. Better still, many universities offer training and mediation services when there are strikes in many industries. What about offering these to their own institutions? Or it is a case of 'the isangoma doesn't diagnose and heal a family member'?

We are not blind, Comrade Dave. We see these double standards.

Now let us get more political.

I argue that Wits, Rhodes, the University of Cape Town (UCT) and Stellenbosch in particular are deeply entrenched in the cycle of global neo-liberal elitism, whose hierarchy is based on race and gender. This produces undesirable outcomes for the students.

These institutions are chasing global ratings, spending huge resources trying to complete or match the Ivy League institutions of North America and Europe. This hampers their ability to deal constructively with local issues or, as Marxists would say, they miss the contemporary moment. The upside of chasing global ratings is that graduates of Wits, UCT, Stellenbosch and other universities can boast about their alma mater believing this increases their chances in the global labour market. It also promotes the work of researchers. The downside, however, is that these institutions are missing the point: they are making a leap before they set a solid base from which to address the lack of transformation, resolve students' grievances and make these universities more relevant and responsive to the national development agenda. That is why university spaces are bureaucratised and securitised instead of being open public spaces of thought, discourse and learning. You pay to access everything – even research that is publicly funded.

Even worse, those institutions chasing international recognition are actually comparing themselves with the wrong institutions – largely private universities in North America and Europe that have billions in endowments. Also, the majority of students who study at Yale, Harvard, the London School of Economics and Oxford are on full scholarships. Therefore, the costs of an education in these Ivy League institutions are not an issue for those gaining an education from there.

Finally, chasing membership of the neo-liberal league has seen the transplanting of the commercialisation of education and all university services; hence students and unions are now saying #InSourceServices. Residences are being turned into self-catering accommodation charged at premium. You have been a student at the University of Johannesburg (UJ) so you know what I am talking about. Just look at what commercialisation has done to tertiary institutions in Australia. Just as well that guy is no longer Prime Minister there: the fellow was privatising higher education, making the fees unaffordable for poor students.

Another issue is that not all of the money being spent on so-called top academics is good value for money. Some are just nice to have in the profiles of faculties and the costs are passed on to the students. And before I forget, Comrade Dave, I have sat on countless interviewing panels since I became a senior manager at the ripe old age of 26. I am not in a position to confirm that Wits, UCT, Stellenbosch and Rhodes graduates are more competent than graduates from Limpopo and Fort Hare. Parents are charged top dollar but students from UJ and Venda are equally hungry for success and very competitive. At least in government we don't patronise them like the private sector and send them on countless training programmes which are meant to keep them in the junior ranks. We hire them and they deliver even though their degrees cost half of what our 'Ivy Leagues' charge.

Then, there is this insidious thing called academic freedom. It is a very perverted thing. In Canada for example, the state regulates the percentage by which universities can increase fees. The range is about 4%. Public universities also don't hypocritically claim academic freedom. They fully appreciate that they are public institutions with a developmental mandate. Should we take seriously people who increase fees by 12% when their workers are told to moderate their salary demands to below the 6% inflation rate?

Should we shake their hands when they increase fees so late in the year that even students with bursaries will end up having shortfalls as their sponsors would have already made their financial commitments for the forthcoming year? Should we really just keep quiet because if the state intervenes it will violate the principles of academic freedom? No, Dave, I tend to differ. I call this perversion because it is not consistently applied.

I remain confused about why these universities can't creatively leverage their positions to mobilise capital for all their students. They can use their large endowments and access to social capital in South Africa and international multinational companies where their funders and former students work. They can leverage National Student Financial Aid Scheme funding to raise millions from the financial market.

This is a schizophrenia that is playing itself out with students at the margins. The rate of commercialisation is greater than the state-funding increases and has long passed what bursaries can afford too. The African National Congress spokesperson is correct: fee increases are anti-black. Whatever the motivation for these excessive increases, the consequence is that children from poor and middle-class black families are negatively affected – and now white lower-middle-class households are affected as well. We judge the outcomes not the intention.

Before I forget, I hope you are paying attention to the level of diversity and maturity displayed by these sons and daughters of the revolution. They are breaking all racial and gender stereotypes. There is political tolerance and unity of action. Faculties that study society need to take a closer look. They are smart kids motivated by one thing: to fight injustice. And then the police decide to make them martyrs by bungling them into police vans. They take pictures with their smartphones and post them on social media and public opinion turns in their favour. Now that is smart politicking, Dave.

Be well, my friend, and remember those #TranformTukkies activists look up to you as a former student leader there.

The University of Pretoria, DASO and my role as a student leader after the 2016 student protests

Akhona Mdunge

I AM A SECOND YEAR Bachelor of Laws student at the University of Pretoria (UP). I am an active political member of the Democratic Alliance Student Organisation (DASO) at the university, having served on their general committees pertaining to residence and race transformation, their law unit and as their vice secretary for a brief stint. At the time of writing this essay, I have since stepped down as their vice secretary to take up the role of the study finances official in the student representative council. The views that will be expressed in this essay do not reflect the views and opinions of neither the UP SRC or DASO UP.

This essay will contribute to the views as presented through my analysis of how I have experienced student politics in and around the University of Pretoria. I will begin by providing my take of the #AfrikaansMustFall movement followed by an analysis of the strikes that broke out at Pretoria High School for Girls. I will conclude by giving an opinion as to why more needs to be done by universities to stimulate students.

Shortly after the 2016 academic year commenced at the University of Pretoria, protest action aimed at addressing the issues of language of instruction and learning quickly gained momentum under the hashtag #AfrikaansMustFall. A lot can be said and indeed a lot was said during the protests about this movement. Not very much has been said about the role that Afriforum played but that will be an analysis for another essay.

I will confirm that all the protests that I have taken part in and experienced at the UP almost always tends to be characteristically split between different races. Certain race groups are hell-bent on maintaining the status quo and resisting any actions that even rhyme with transformation. This blocking against anything that seeks to make the university more inclusive is sponsored and I do hope that the judgement that seeks to reveal private donors of political organisations is upheld so that we know who funds student political organisation on campuses during SRC campaigns and elections. They utilise this financial strength to hinder transformative progress whilst creating areas of white Afrikaner exclusivity.

The movements at UP have never been an attack on Afrikaner culture but rather they posed very important questions about the realities of the country considering its history as well as the university's future as a university in Africa in an inclusive democratic South Africa. Amongst other things, the #AfrikaansMustFall movement questioned the financial viability of Afrikaans as a language of instruction especially when one takes into account the declining numbers of Afrikaans students versus the overwhelmingly growing number of black African students attending this historically Afrikaans university.

The movement raised the issue of the need to cut down on university expenditure so as to better assist financially needy black students but still maintain a balanced financial statement at the end of the financial year. I remember one of my lecturers telling me about how the university decided to revamp all the signage across the whole university and keep it all in Afrikaans, which was when they realised the pressure to change was against the Afrikaans powers that be, which cost millions of rands.

The movement also spoke of the plight of black students in finding a place and space in the university in such a way that felt they belonged in a country in which they are an overwhelming majority. To this day I struggle to comprehend why a strike by university students, who should be focused on their academics, was needed to pressurise lecturers and professors into realising that Afrikaans was not a conducive language of study at the university. Ignorance, racism, exclusivity and privilege of white academics celebrates itself in white university spaces, violently so. More recently, I have also begun to wonder whether there is any link between the high dropout rate and failure of black students from UP purposely driven by these white racist lecturers.

If one looks closely, it's very easy to see a correlation between the #AfrikaansMustFall movement and the strike at Pretoria Girls High School (PGHS) where black students were protesting to be allowed to wear their hair any way they chose without white standards of beauty and neatness being imposed on them using the excuse of school culture. Both movements were about our identity as black people, about educating the white minority to stop imposing their archaic European culture in Africa and about affirming the humanity of all black Africans. This rise in attitude amongst high school and university students about being proud of being black speaks directly to the Black Consciousness of black leaders who led the youth movement in the 1970s.

Throughout the period in which I, along with several other black students, was protesting the university's language policy, I had not become a member of DASO-UP, and I was very apolitical. The movement had largely been led by SASCO and EFFSC student body affiliates. However, neither DASO-UP leadership, nor its supporters had been present during the protest. The organisation had opted to commence discussions with management structures at the university with the aim of finding a presumably less radical manner to address the pertinent issue.

To understand DASO, one must first understand its support base. This understanding stems purely from my observations. Many of the students that vote for DASO have minimal interest in student – or national politics. These students are largely academically driven and never want their institutions of higher learning to be shut down for any reasons especially ones which are of interest to the black student populous. Some vote for the student party because of the non-radical approach it has taken over the years to find solutions to problems. One must note that DASO has received backlash for their approach from other political student organisations at UP and across other university campuses across the country.

Once, during a recruitment drive of students for DASO on campus, I was told by one student that the DA student organisation is 'too nowhere when shit hits the fan'. I must stress, though, that the party does not receive its mandate as to how to proceed with its modus operandi from the parent political organisation. It must also be noted that DASO continued to actively participate in the language policy work streams and made recommendations that have since been adopted by the university.

Political student organisations at UP also detest DASO's absence from movements like #FeesMustFall. During 2015/2016's Fees Must Fall protests, DASO-UP and its members were not involved in the shutting down of the university's operations. It, however, opted to go to Church Square where, working together with other provincial DASO bodies, it marched to the National Treasury with the intention of questioning the finance minister, Pravin Gordhan, and other provincial finance council members as to what the plans were in their budget planning for the funding for poor and underprivileged students' tuition fees.

A few elements of DASO-UP were further seen during the protest at PGHS. Radical activism at DASO is not as traditionally defined as it is amongst other political student organisations. But radical activism is not the mandate that the party's leadership receives from its supporters. As much as I have at times become frustrated at the party's lack of activism, I have come to appreciate the strides that the party makes to address pertinent student problems and realised the concept that the party leadership acts as agents through a mandate given by its mandator (the support base) as guided by the party's constitution.

With that said, however, DASO-UP does not, for example, receive its mandate from the Democratic Alliance. Both parent and student organisations have been at loggerheads about how to tackle issues many times. The extent of the independence of the student organisation must be emphasised in this respect. I'll illustrate this with an example. When the recent Heher report on the feasibility of higher education was released, the DA was quick to accept many of the recommendations. National DASO went on record and rejected the aforesaid recommendations. The DA has since changed its stance on the report. Ours is not to blindly accept approaches, ideologies or instructions from the DA as DASO-UP. DASO is under no obligation to endorse statements from the DA if their constituents – the youth – do not agree with the parent body.

Afrikaans remains a language of instruction at the university and will do so for first-year students until 2019 due to hindrances caused by legal action to prevent the university scrapping Afrikaans as a language of instruction. The question that I want to analyse in this regard is whether this victory was brought about by the radical activism of the political parties that led the #AfrikaansMustFall movement or whether it was bought about through the concerted efforts of organisations like the DASO to present reasonable and workable solutions to the university's stakeholders. I have come to realise the importance that the university attaches to its image, presumably for investment reasons.

The #AfrikaansMustFall movement caused a negative image for the university as the strike action was broadcasted across national media, sparking public outrage and condemnation that Afrikaans remained a language of instruction at the historically Afrikaans university. Although this mass action was not as sustainable, it played a pivotal role in creating cognisance as to the urgency of the problem. I can speak very little of the conversations about the issue that were being had before my arrival at the university in 2016, but I can speak to the immediate impact that was had by the radical activism of the mass action.

DASO-UP was actively and publicly involved in the #AfrikaansMustFall protests and was visibly protesting the PGHS hair policy, albeit in their small numbers, it was resoundingly voted into university student leadership by their supporters. I submit that this act should serve as a ratification of the supporters of the issues that the DASO-UP leadership has addressed and their approach to addressing these issues in this regard. I only lament the lack of political activism by DASO supporters and do concede that more still needs to be done by the party to stimulate political student activism amongst its support base to create forums for the discussion and understanding of important societal issues that impact many students of diverse backgrounds.

Many university students continue to graduate without a trace of social consciousness. In a country like ours where we have a deep history of racial, cultural and gender prejudice, young people, especially those with the privilege of attending university, should prioritise educating themselves to be conscious of their positions in society at present and the history that shaped their present. In the absence of hunger for social consciousness, we all, too often, find ourselves in a situation where movements like #FeesMustFall are opposed by those who simply 'do not understand why they are striking again'.

This is the impasse in which we currently find ourselves. When students demand curriculum transformation and decolonisation, it is precisely because they have seen the gap in how knowledge is produced and distributed. The absence of an accurate account of the history and African context in our education system prevents social progress.

Until such a time comes, we take stock of our challenges and we accept as South Africans that we can only move forward together, where we are united on the issue of a free university, the curriculum, cultural and institutional transformation. If we truly value our country, we should be able to find strength in our diversity as South Africans and to engage honestly with each other. The issue of over-excessive radicalism on one side and white arrogance on the other only sees the country moving in circles rather than forward.

Must we die young?

Nkateko Mabasa

In 2000, when I was just eight years old, the world was supposed to end. The millennium computer bug (Y2K) was allegedly going to infiltrate computers and cause the world to shut down. But it didn't. Then in 2008, when I was 15, a black man became the president of America. Suddenly this world, that was supposed to have ended, became big and wide, and full of possibilities. These are the makings of a millennial.

After the fall of apartheid in 1994, South Africa was determined to rebuild itself. Men and women whom for years knew nothing but pain and violence could now reach those dreams borne in suffering. President Nelson Mandela stood tall as a leader who could be trusted, a force of moral authority, who had suffered and overcome. He bore the hopes of his country on his shoulders, as well as its internal frustrations.

People who were traumatised for years in their communities had to decide whether to act on that anger or to choose a different path for a much-needed respite from death. The world had been swept by this news. They were inspired by this giant of a man, who spent 27 years in prison, and somehow had love for his enemies. This is the world that witnessed the Sharpeville massacre in 1960 and decided to mourn with South Africa by declaring 21 March as International Human Rights Day.

Across the borders, they, too, were coming out of years of war. The Cold War had finally been won by the fall of communism.

When Gorbachev decided to resign and disintegrate the Soviet Union, liberal democracy had won. Generation X had defeated the world's problems – wars, racism and communism. Technological advancement would also defeat famine, disease and change the nature of work all together.

The world was marching, and South Africa would embrace this wave of development and globalisation. It would integrate itself into the world market, fostering economic dependency across nations to discourage conflict. You can't wage war on a nation you import resources from. Democracy would birth out the New Man, who would be free to pursue his own plans, stretch out into the world without colour, class or gender standing in the way. A person would be not be judged by the colour of his or her skin but their character. It is this ethos that millennials see in their parents. A generation that stood up and fought, that resisted and rebelled and finally rose to the mountain top. Generation X embraced the company office. Finally, black men and women would enter the blue-collar work force.

And yet, we live at a time where the digital revolution is slowly reducing the labour force. Factories are closing and conventional work spaces are changing. With just an iPhone alone, one can make a living at the comfort of their own home. No wonder, we the youth, experience an existential dilemma as we go out into the world. The lessons taught at home almost seem obsolete.

With this episode of history, coupled with a compromised democracy, at the height of chaos and a liberation euphoria, millennials seemed lost, confused and aimless. And yet our vision is clear and far reaching. We are well aware of the sharp edges and the cruel and indifferent nature of the white-supremacist, capitalist, patriarchal super-structure that was supposed to have been defeated. It has only reinvented itself, disguised as a postcolonial world, but still employing the same methods of exploitation and disenfranchisement. Dark and lonesome is that day, when the millennial discovers, much to her disbelief, that she is black, and the world still thinks it matters.

Life is best lived with some kind of meaning. When you are 50 years old and fast approaching the end, you look back more into the past, to gather the pieces of actions, spread out wide, aimlessly, so as to extract some purpose – a reason for one's suffering. Our elders cannot accept a South Africa that is not yet Uhuru. What has become of their efforts and sacrifice, and years of exile and resistance? Was it all for nothing?

As students we have decided to see the world as it is – oppressive and anti-black. We have made our path to consciousness. We have seen that being black in South Africa is a mark of shame, coupled with poverty and landlessness. As students, we have experienced the disenfranchisement; the criminal act of having our personhood defined by others; and the constant, relentless and debilitating fear that gives 'no rest at night, no peace at dawn', brought only by being 'custodians of the black body'.

We have seen the false promises of colonial education, an education that has rendered the African spirit to slip into a 'deep pessimism of despair'. We have seen our mothers and fathers and those who have come before us suffer a merciless death: not a physical one but a death of the African personality, to be no more than hollow empty shells and robbed of all individuality. Broken by the barbarous system that disguises itself as a liberal education, our forefathers have met their end at these heinous crimes that have been created to feed the abhorrent beast that is white supremacy.

Never has there been a more pressing issue for this generation to tackle and overcome. It goes at the very heart of self-determination. The colonial ward has finally decided to remove the shackles of exploitation, to awake from the long 'slumber of monotony', to create an awareness of self that breaks the low row of weary thoughts: the cognitive dissonance of being black and innocent.

At this, we arrived by being witness to the disappointed hopes of our parents, who thought these institutions of higher learning would emancipate them and us from poverty. Here we are as their children saying, 'We are still poor!' Our parents made one mistake which we must not. The rainbow dream of democracy made them forget that they are black, and it is this very blackness which is the cause of their suffering.

We see in them our future – the arduous and seemingly inescapable path they took, the path that kills one's personality and the path which seems predestined for us to follow. And so, with these blatant truths that face us, as their children, the youth and students, a question gnaws at the deep crevices of our consciousness. We are forced to cry out with the most solemn of contemplation: Must we die young? Must we accept our lot? Must we bury who we are to some place so deep so as not to upset whiteness? Must we disguise our black souls? This treacherous beast, that is white supremacy, would have us be no more than clogs in its capitalist machinery. Must we allow ourselves to be slaves again, with no ambitions and aspirations, without hope. Must we die young?

Reflections on #FeesMustFall in the wake of the passing of Professor Bongani Mayosi

Sibusiso Chalufu

THE STORY OF THE EXPERIENCES of Professor Bongani Mayosi at the hands of student activists at the University of Cape Town (UCT) – which, according to the *Sunday Times* of 5 August 2018, where his sister called it 'the vandalisation of his soul by the #FeesMustFall students' – has reopened deep wounds which have not fully healed. Apart from Mayosi's passing reigniting debate about a number of issues, including depression and the associated stigma, particularly in the black community, this has also brought back the debate about the treatment of staff, particularly black staff, in our institutions of higher learning.

Whether or not the #FeesMustFall movement contributed to the demise of this eminent scholar, humble giant and true epitome of black excellence, is debatable – and to be sure, there has been vibrant public discourse about this question since his death last week. But that is not what this brief reflective piece aims to focus on.

A lot has been written about the 2015/2016 period of major upheavals at our higher education institutions in South Africa. Experiences of students and student leaders are well documented – including through a brilliant play, *The Fall*, by UCT drama graduates. Experiences of university vice chancellors have also been eloquently captured in a recent book by Professor Jonathan Jansen, *As By Fire:*

The End of the South African University. Coincidentally, Jansen has also reflected on Mayosi's experiences and those of other university managers during that tumultuous period.

Very little, if anything, is known about the experiences of the administrative and professional support staff at the hands of the legitimately angry, aggrieved and highly frustrated young people (mostly black) at our universities and colleges. These administrative and professional support staff are the very individuals who are always closest to the students and closest to the fire. I am talking specifically about the student affairs and services practitioners who, at times, go out of their way to assist students, including from their own personal resources; who provide support to incarcerated students beyond the call of duty, without making a song and dance about it; who have had to go against university rules of not supporting arrested protesting students – doing so because, despite everything that these students may or may not have done, at the end of the day, they are our young people who need us and who should still be supported and guided throughout their growth and development into adulthood.

These are individuals who have suffered in silence, who have been targeted, attacked, dehumanised, used and abused; individuals who have experienced the wrath of students at its worst, at times without understanding why. These individuals found themselves between the university and students, with very little support from the university, and have borne the heaviest brunt than most people care to acknowledge.

On Sunday, 13 September 2015, just before midnight, while away at home in Pretoria on leave, I received a frantic call from the head of risk management services (what in some institutions is referred to as campus protection services) of the University of KwaZulu-Natal (UKZN). From his strained voice I could immediately tell that something was seriously amiss. He informed me that the university administration block had been attacked and burned by a group of about 20 students and pleaded with me to come back. As it turned out, this was just the start as a few minutes later the risk management services building and the CCTV room were also attacked and burned by the same group of students. I duly flew back and went to campus early the following morning on 14 September 2015.

On the night of Tuesday, 15 September 2015 at 22:25, a group of about 12 students attacked and petrol-bombed the university flat in the O-Block residence where I was temporarily residing. The university flat was burned to ashes and the only reason I was not was because a young man who was by then the manager of student governance and leadership development, Meliqiniso Sibisi, advised me against sleeping at the flat. A part of me had seriously considered ignoring his advice because, as I reasoned then, in my more than 15 years' working with students, I had never had any reason to fear them – in fact, I had been in a number of extremely volatile situations, including where I had to face and address large masses of extremely angry students, single-handedly. So, I seriously had no fear at all.

But nothing could have prepared me for what was clearly a personal attack and an attempt on my life. Apart from feeling gutted, instead of being angry with the students, I was left with questions as to why would students consider me a target for such a brutal attack?

Perhaps the questions shouldn't have arisen given the fact that there had previously been a number of inexplicable attacks, including an attack on our disability support unit offices and the burning down of a vehicle we had purchased to transport students with disabilities. So, there was nothing special about the executive director for student services, who therefore would not have been spared from such attack.

Apart from dealing with constant nightmares, the loss of some personal valuables and the inconvenience of having to use different vehicles as a safety measure, including the use of a university-rented vehicle, I haven't taken time to reflect on the effects of what happened to me – the toll that it took both on me and on my family – nor did I attend any counselling.

Perhaps what may have assisted me is that it did not take long for me to forgive the students who had attempted to kill me, even as I was still grappling with all kinds of feelings and unanswered questions. In fact, a few days later, I was back working with the student leaders, including those I suspected, and had been reliably informed, were behind the attempt on my life.

I would venture to argue that my situation, after this traumatic incident, is not unique but rather is symptomatic of the experiences of many student affairs and services practitioners at our institutions. There has been select instances of institutions offering support to their staff, including counselling services and debriefing sessions, but for the most part, there hasn't been any concerted and systematic support for staff aimed at dealing with the day-to-day challenges that they face, for whom the experiences of 2015/2016 was a culmination of years of dehumanising pain and suffering, mostly at the hands of the students.

The fact that not much is known or has been written about the painful experiences of administrative and professional support staff, is quite unfortunate – this, notwithstanding the nature and the type of work that characterises the lives of student affairs and services practitioners in our institutions, which leaves very little room for taking a step back and engaging in critical reflection.

Beyond the documenting of the experiences of student affairs and services practitioners, there is a need for critical reflection on the events of 2015/2016, with a view to extrapolating critical lessons to guide us into the future. We need to ask ourselves whether we could have done better in the manner in which we as universities – particularly as student affairs and services practitioners – dealt with the #FeesMustFall period. Should we perhaps have pledged greater solidarity with the students; could we have worked closely with student leaders even as we were most often targets of attacks or seen as the enemy?

Is there more that could have been done? How else could we have contributed to the legitimate student struggles for transformation and free higher education? Are there any lessons that were learned from what transpired during the 2015/2016 period in our institutions? Did we or have we done enough to know who our students are and to develop an understanding of where they come from, what they seek and what contribution we can make towards all that?

These and other questions still require critical reflection and, perhaps most importantly, they require us to develop and design an agenda for transformation that is both responsive and forward looking.

First published by Daily Maverick, *14 August 2018. Available at: https://www.dailymaverick.co.za/opinionista/2018-08-14-reflections-on-feesmustfall-in-the-wake-of-the-passing-of-prof-bongani-mayosi/*

To be a decolonial born again

Sabelo J. Ndlovu-Gatsheni

THESE DAYS I HAVE ADOPTED a pentecostal pastoral methodology in my scholarship. It is a practical methodology that enables me to call out demons of coloniality where ever they are hiding within us. It works through loud calling as a form of exorcism:

1. Demon of racism come out,
2. Demon of patriarchy and sexism come out,
3. Demon of tribalism and regionalism come out,
4. Demon of xenophobia and Afrophobia come out,
5. Demon of epistemic xenophobia come out,
6. Demon of imperialism come out,
7. Demon of epistemic deafness come out,
8. Demon of hatred and evil come out,
9. Demon of jealousy come out,
10. Demon of ukudelela come out.

I then call on the therapeutic and liberatory decolonial love to embrace us, heal us, comfort us and remember us as new human beings: The decolonial born agains.

Amen!

PART 4
THE HIGHER EDUCATION POLICY QUAGMIRE

University transformation re-imagined: Discourses resulting after the Fallist movements

Mabone Lerato Kgosiemang

The Fees Must Fall movement, the Rhodes Must Fall movement and other Fallists movements have played a critical role in facilitating new conversations in the boardrooms, lecture halls and corridors of several universities. As a result of these movements, some conversations that were relegated to the corridors because of inequality have now been inserted into boardroom and staff-meeting agendas. One of these conversations is the critique of university transformation processes. For the first time since 1994, universities are critically engaging with the limits of transformation and reimagining possibilities for deeper change that might come as a result of decolonisation. This essay provides a discussion of such critiques as shared by students from the University of Johannesburg.

THE FEES MUST FALL and the Rhodes Must Fall movements played a significant role in creating debates and discussion within higher education. Students, historically, have been instrumental agents of change. As it became clear that the 2015 student struggles were escalating, people like Xolela Mangcu were making public comments that if the voices of students were not heard, there was a possibility that things could get out of hand. The Fees Must Fall movement and Rhodes Must Fall movement emerged from frustrations felt by students within higher education. This was because the higher education space maintained its colonial legacies, which made students feel excluded, ignored and frustrated (Naidoo, 2016). Luescher-Mamashela (2011) shows that when students perceive that they are not being heard, protest action becomes inevitable.

From 1994 the need for transformation in higher education has become a common conversation, with government placing policies such as the Education White Paper 3: A Programme for the Transformation of Higher Education Act 101 of 1997 towards it. The changes that came as a result of this Act and the activities of universities did not satisfy students. Students argue that the discourse of transformation was shallow and felt that much broader and deeper structural changes were needed. Thus, the students challenged the authorities and changed the dialogue to the radical notion of decolonisation.

The Fallist movements amplified the voices and activism of students. Activists like Mahapa (2015) argued that higher education failed to listen; even in its transformation agenda, it remained inhabitable for the majority of students as it remained a colonial space. Similarly, Naidoo (2016: 183) had argued that transformation discourses need to be done away with completely as they are too superficial and fail to address deeper colonial, structural issues. Students were ready to dismantle the higher education space and decolonise it.

This essay begins by looking at some of the discussions and dialogues on the Fees Must Fall movement. It further gives the methodological processes that informed the study. The essay then articulates those discussions brought forward by students that have changed the discourse on higher education. Finally, this chapter concludes and summarises the changes within higher education brought on by the Fees Must Fall movement.

Methodology
This essay is derived from my master's dissertation, which used the qualitative research method. This method allowed me to gain in-depth descriptive information from the participants, who gave an insider's perspective as Fees Must Fall leaders from the University of the Witwatersrand (Wits). The participants were purposefully selected as social actors, as relevant student activists. Through one-

on-one interviews with nine participants detailed, rich information pertaining to their experiences and perceptions of the Fees Must Fall movement and discussions within the higher education landscape was collected (Kumar, 2005). However, this chapter is based on the experiences shared by five participants.

All of the study participants were African and had first-hand experiences of the transformation discussions and narratives at Wits. The interviews allowed participants to express themselves and probing was used to facilitate deeper discussion. Thematic analysis was used for data analysis and for the creation and linking of themes and ideas emerging from the data (Matthews & Ross, 2010). The project received ethical clearance from the University of Johannesburg Faculty of Humanities ethics committee. Again, the names of participants used in this chapter are pseudonyms.

Transformation out, we are talking decolonisation now

Eradicating the legacy of colonisation and apartheid remains one of the primary tasks of uniting and developing South Africa. The Department of Education (1997) saw this as a necessity and thus positioned itself to do the same within higher education. Badat (2010: 2) shows that the government wants to create a higher education landscape that is a 'democratic, non-racial, non-sexist system'. This fits well to the explanation of transformation by Legoabe (2011: 1) who says it must have the following qualities: it must be non-racial, non-sexist, united and democratic.

These discussions and understanding of transformation existed before the Fees Must Fall movements and often dominated discourses envisioned for the future of South Africa. However, the Fees Must Fall movement problematised this; they argued that the imperatives in the university transformation principles were not enough to create equality. Tshegofatso, a feminist and former student representative council member, explained this issue thus: 'It's a form of redressing something that would have happened in the past and not necessarily reversing it but to redress it' (Tshegofatso, female, 30 January 2017).

Contrary to the Department of Education (1997), Tshegofatso does not believe that the transformation of higher education will systematically eradicate the colonial legacy. She raises concerns that the structures will remain intact and that remedying the historical injustices without deconstructing and eradicating the foundations will not bring equality. Similarly, Bongani, an Economic Freedom Fighter and Black Consciousness advocate, argues: 'Transformation for me is, is really, not, it's trying to change something, but not completely, not a 360 degree turn. But merely making it suitable for everyone, to sort of adapt to it' (Bongani, male, 24 November 2016).

'Not a 360-degree turn' is how Bongani sees transformation. He also argues that it is 'trying to change something', but not really succeeding. The idea raised by Legoabe (2011: 1) and Badat (2010: 2) about higher education and the government viewing creation of a 'non-racial, non-sexist, united and democratic' space is seen as a means of altering higher education. Bongani shows that the discussions that existed prior to the Fees Must Fall movement, even though necessary for making higher education equal, were not adequate. The discussion of transformation failed to see that without fundamental change, transformation policies and activities failed to be really inclusive and by making people adapt, it may force assimilation into the institutions as they currently are. Notwithstanding the arguments by the two participants, Nkoane (2006) and Lebakeng, Phalane & Dalindjebo (2006) had begun questioning and conversing on the flaws of transformation and the need for decolonial thought before the Fallists movements. Albeit these studies and conversations did not gain the popular support and influence at the time unlike the Fallist movements.

The discussions on transformation failed to resonate within the Fees Must Fall movement. It's very conceptualisation was found to be problematic and unsubstantial; therefore, it needed to fall away as a point of departure. Sifiso, a non-partisan and Pan-Africanist student activist points out the following:

> I actually do not believe in transformation number one. I believe transformation, how it is conceptualised in the university, it is a game of numbers. Where we are changing white faces with black faces and to me that is not the solution to our condition as black people in these universities. Because now we could have 10 white people and replace them with 10 black people. How is that going to change our condition? (Sifiso, male, 17 March 2017)

Sifiso sees transformation as a numbers game, which he is critical of as nothing really changes apart from the racial and gender make-up of the university. The underlying, deeper discussions about what makes higher education habitable for all remains untouched and a false notion of progress arises. Even though it is important that the gender and racial make-up of universities be addressed, it is pivotal that the conversations and ideological underpinnings of universities also shift.

The shifting conversation as a result of the Fallist movement is clearly one that suggests that transformation of higher education failed when it came to the things that counted. For example, Paseka, a strong decolonial Fanonian activist and part of the Economic Freedom Fighters Students Command leadership, argues the following:

> Transformation to me is a failing project in post-apartheid South Africa; this is why we speak of a 'post-apartheid, apartheid South Africa'. Because if you look at the infrastructure of apartheid, the inequalities they are still intact and the governing party right now it is gatekeeping for white Afrikaners, Boers. Who stole our land, and are now ruling us in the land of our own birth? So, transformation I think was a language that was manipulated by the liberation movement comrades of the ANC ... Transformation even, if you think about it, philosophically, it means take what is there and try to change it and make it better. Right, which has been established by many scholars, by your Bikos, by your Fanons, right, that it's not a project that is for us black people. We are meant to be the ones that are at the bottom of the food chain, anyone can oppress us, and anything can happen and even when you are alive or dead you do not have the self-determination (Paseka, male, 27 January 2017).

Paseka raises a concern that discussions raised under the transformation banner are not enough, and it will never be enough to liberate black people. Rather expanding on Manganyi (1976: 5), Paseka argues that the black condition within higher education and the broader society remains the same even after transformation has taken place. The idea and dialogue is too narrowly conceptualised and allows the philosophical and intellectual make-up of the colonial state and higher education to remain intact. Therefore, transformational legislation and engagement has deceived people to believe change will take place while it is a futile exercise that will never succeed as it makes blacks the gatekeepers of the system of their own oppression.

With the emergence of the Fees Must Fall movement and the deconstruction of transformation, the ideological conversations and development of decolonial debates within South African higher education ensued. With the insertion of decolonial thinking and discourses as a result of the Fallist movement, transformation debates began to shift in ways that emphasised how oppressions are linked. Sifiso makes the following argument to illustrate:

> How do I put this? Fees Must Fall, if you are a Fallist, if you believe in Fallism, Fees Must Fall basically means a fall of all these oppressive systems that are perpetuated on the black populace. So, for me if we were to link Fees Must Fall and transformation, Fees Must Fall would say transformation itself must fall. We cannot be talking transformation, transformation must fall we are moving, we are talking decolonisation now. So, in Fees Must Fall, the language of transformation has disappeared, we are speaking decolonisation (Sifiso, male, 17 March 2017).

The Fees Must Fall movement has broken down the very political conceptualisation of higher education. Sifiso shows that there is a shift of conversations within higher education with the development of the student movement. Mahapa (2015) positions the Rhodes Must Fall movement's ideas as decolonising and realigning themselves rather than as limited transformation dialogues and activities. Sifiso argues that discussions of decolonisation are able to unpack and reorganise concepts that have been left in existence with transformation. Those oppressive colonial systems needed to be addressed in a deeper manner than transformation has. The conception and contestation of decolonisation has taken place within higher education as this becomes a key conversation and shift in philosophical and socio-political debate post the multiple Fees Must Fall mass actions. However, the contextualisation for Sibusiso, an international master's student, is explored thus:

Decolonisation for me is a movement or it is a term used by current movements which seeks to critique modernity through attaching the decoloniality perspective, which means it's reinventing basically what has been influenced by colonialism (Sibusiso, male, 10 October 2016).

The explanation by Sibusiso shows us that there is deep intellectual thought behind the debates and dialogues that the Fees Must Fall movement raises. It questions how modernity as a philosophical tool conceptualised the colonial world. This argument interrogates the entire perception of existence and being within the modern era. The dialogue builds on the ideas of thinkers such as Fanon, Biko and Ani, which show that the colonial world structures are in all facets of life. Decolonial thought and decolonisation are an intellectual, academic and socio-political process that humanises the colonised. It facilitates a rethinking of the world, it reconstructs existence as it is known through debates and brings about new intellectual thought.

Conclusion

This essay argues that one of the results of the Fallist movement's debates about the limits of transformation of higher education was that the issues around transformation were debated openly and in public for the first time. Given how the Fallist movement has provided voice to the voiceless and has influenced change in many spaces, including the insourcing of workers, it is no surprise that the notion of transformation has been placed on the agenda as a limited, colonial, patriarchal and capitalist concept that has not fundamentally changed universities. Decolonisation emerges as a point of departure to reimagine the world and rethink conversations within higher education and broader society.

References

Ani, C.N. 2013. 'Appraisal of African epistemology in the global system', *Alternation*, 20(1): 295–320.

Badat, S. 2010. *The Challenges of Transformation in Higher Education and Training Institutions in South Africa*. Johannesburg: Development Bank of Southern Africa.

Biko, S. 2004. *Steve Biko, 1946–1977: I Write What I Like*. Cambridge: ProQuest LLC.

Department of Education. 1997. *White Paper 3 - A Programme for Higher*

Education Transformation. Pretoria: Department of Education.
Fanon, F. 1963. *The Wretched of the Earth*. New York: Grove Press.
Kumar, R. 2005. *Research Methodology*. London: Sage Publications.
Lebakeng, T.J., M.M. Phalane & N. Dalindjebo. 2006. 'Epistemicide, institutional cultures and the imperative for the Africanisation of universities in South Africa', *Alternation*, 13(1): 70–87.
Legoabe, R. 2011. 'The role of students and alumni in higher education transformation'. Discussion paper prepared for the Anti-Racism Network in Higher Education Colloqium, University of Johannesburg, 27 May 2011.
Luescher-Mamashela, T. M. 2011. *Student Involvement in University Decision-making: Good Reasons, a New Lens*. Cape Town: Taylor & Francis.
Mahapa, R. 2015. 'Letter to SRC presidents by Ramabina Mahapa (UCT SRC president)'. Available at: http://www.uct.ac.za/dailynews/?id=9133. Accessed on 1 September 2016.
Manganyi, N. C. 1976. *Being-Black-in-the-World*. Johannesburg: Ravan Press.
Matthews, B. & L. Ross. 2010. *Research Methods: A Practical Guide for the Social Sciences*. Essex: Pearson Education.
Naidoo, L. 2016. 'Contemporary student politics in South Africa: The rise of the black-led student movements #RhodesMustFall and #FeesMustFall in 2015', in A. Heffernan & N. Nieftagodien (eds). *Students Must Rise: Youth Struggle in South Africa Before and Beyond Soweto '76*. Johannesburg: Wits University Press.
Nkoane, M. M. 2006. 'The Africanisation of the university in Africa', *Alternation*, 13(1): 49–69.
Seabi, J., J. Seedat & K. Khoza-Shangase. 2014. 'Experiences of university students regarding transformation in South Africa', *International Journal of Educational Management*, 28(1): 66–81.

Young people shook South Africa to the core: Reflections of the student protests of 2015 and beyond

Imraan Buccus

RHODES MUST FALL and Fees Must Fall, along with the Reference List protest at Rhodes University, shook middle-class South Africa to the core. Indeed, this series of protests garnered considerable global attention.

The first phase of protest, which came to be known under the hashtag #RhodesMustFall, emerged alongside the Black Lives Matter movement in the United States and connected with an international impulse towards decolonisation. It was a complicated moment in which important critiques of racist curricula and symbols were mixed in with the often very problematic elements of American identity politics and some forms of home-grown chauvinism.

In a disappointing response, that would continue as protests evolved, commentators tended to be either wholly for or against the protests with people taking nuanced and sophisticated stances. This made evidenced-based and rational discussion very difficult. This problem was compounded by a vicious form of often online authoritarianism and bullying from within the ranks of the protestors themselves.

It has always been the prerogative of youth to challenge their elders and ask new questions. The youth are often a source of intellectual renewal. But for many my age, well aware of the courage and principle of many members of the older generation, some of whom have certainly not 'sold out' in the new order, it was disturbing to see this wholesale dismissal of the achievements of an entire generation. Certainly, the older generation should not enter the discussion with the assumption that their experience and power mean they have all the answers. But at the same time the youth do not have all the answers, and a mutually respectful intergenerational conversation could be very useful.

But the statue of Rhodes did fall, and the normalisation of colonial ideas and practices was dealt a fatal blow. This first wave of protests did issue a significant blow to colonial hegemony.

The second phrase of protest, known under the hashtag #FeesMustFall, was the culmination of a set of struggles, waged mostly in historically black universities (HBUs) since the end of apartheid. This was a moment of mass struggle and the high point of the societal support for student struggles. Access to education is clearly a democratic right and there was, at this point, wide support for the students. That support was soon squandered though by authoritarianism and intolerance from within the movement. It became clear that there was significant penetration of the movement by intelligence agents, and other pro-Zuma and Gupta forces, like Black First, Land First.

In social movement struggles at the grassroots level, known and suspected agents have worked to divide organisations via standard practices such as making false allegations, developing smear campaigns against individuals and the like. It would be naïve to not assume that at least some of the damaging conduct that emerged within the student movement at this point was linked to intelligence. It also seems likely that attempts to push the movement into positions that would result in further crises on campus may well have been linked to attempts by the Zuma/Gupta project to deflect attention away from itself.

But despite all the problems that emerged in the student movement, this phase of the struggle did put the question of free education on the table in a decisive manner. It remains on the table and real progress on this question is quite possible.

At Rhodes University there was a third movement to the student struggles of 2015 and 2016 in form of the #ReferenceList protests in opposition to rape and sexual harassment. This did not become a national movement but it did seem to anticipate the international #MeToo movement that came later.

There was a tremendous amount of hubris among the students and their supporters. This series of struggles was often presented as the arrival of a special generation that would, almost magically, resolve all our problems. The protests certainly did put coloniality, the commodification of education and, at Rhodes, sexual harassment and rape, on the agenda but they also failed in other important respects. For a start they did not succeed in building an enduring movement. In fact, on all campuses the movement quickly collapsed, often amid ugly recriminations. They also failed to build sustained links with struggles off campus. In many campuses, along with significant penetration by intelligence, there was rapid party-political capture and instrumentalisation of the movement. The Zuma/Gupta faction of the ANC and the EFF both worked hard to capture student struggles for their own narrow purposes.

Furthermore, while an urgent set of issues was placed on the table this was often done in a manner that was seriously misguided in terms of how lines of accountability were managed. For instance, on many campuses university managers were viciously attacked over questions relating to fees. Now of course university managers should have been held responsible for their failures to transform the curriculum. But it makes no sense at all to hold university managers responsible for the failure of the state to ensure university access. This inappropriate deflection of blame from the state to university managers was something of a propaganda coup for the Zuma/Gupta faction of the ANC.

There was also a serious failure to link university issues to wider societal issues. For instance, the atrocious state of public schools was not seriously addressed and engaged. And seriously problematic actors within the student movement, including people who made gross anti-Semitic statements and were exceedingly problematic in terms of gender, were not dealt with in an adequate manner. In some instances, the movement collapsed into appalling forms of chauvinism.

In the heat of the movement I wrote an article suggesting ways in which the tumult could be shifted onto a more rational and strategic consideration of the way forward. I argued that there were hard truths to be faced by all sides and have listed a few of these hard truths below.

As Tshepo Motsepe from Equal Education has pointed out, university vice chancellors cannot deliver free education or any kind of structural reform to education funding. It is only the government that can do this. For this reason, protests must be aimed at the government. Students need to take this reality a lot more seriously. The government has failed to prioritise higher education and this needs to change, and quickly. Again, this is something that student activists, some who are ANC aligned, need to take on board. Max Price and Adam Habib have no role in deciding how we allocate our budget.

As academic Nico Cloete has shown, free education for all amounts to a subsidy for the rich. This is because the crisis in our public school system means that most people who get to university come from well-to-do families. The call for free education across the board is therefore seriously misguided. Education should be free for the poor, there should be modest fees for the middle class and the rich should pay at a much higher rate. All actors in this debate need to ensure that their policy proposals are backed by solid research.

This must include a careful comparative examination of how different policies have worked in different countries.

As Nomalanga Mkhize argued, while universities cannot be held accountable for the failure of the state to invest in higher education they must be held accountable for the failure to transform some institutions (UCT, Stellenbosch and Rhodes in particular), the corruption in the system (recently reported at Zululand but a reality elsewhere too) and the drive towards a more commodified and bureaucratised system. Universities need to be honest about their failings.

Academic Jane Duncan has pointed out that calling the police and private security to deal with protest escalates the situation rather than defusing or resolving it. Every effort must be made to choose negotiation over violence. Most violence has come from the police. But a worker at Wits may have died as a result of student action. If this is the case it is disgraceful. Students also need to take responsibility for moving their struggle towards non-violent strategies.

Many commentators have argued the most urgent crisis in our education system is in our schools. Universities cannot fix this or make up for it. The national focus on universities is a welcome development but our schools require the same attention.

Equal Education should get the same media attention as student politics, given the significance of their work and the fact that many of their leaders are former student leaders.

As a few writers have noted, the conflict that has emerged in our universities is an expression of a deeper economic crisis. Universities cannot be expected to somehow compensate for a declining economy that continues to shed jobs. The ruling party doesn't seem to have a plan to get our economy working. This needs to change and very fast too. If we don't get our economy working the crisis in the universities could spread to other parts of society.

The students have failed to link their struggles to trade unions and social movements off campus. This is a serious political failing and has reduced possibilities for solidarity and, also, for building a broad movement for progressive change.

If students want to win wider support, they need to confront and deal with the authoritarian elements in their struggle. The stabbing of the SRC president at Zululand university, locking security in a burning building, the threats to the media and the harassment of other students and staff is unacceptable. It is also not strategic as this is not the way to win friends and influence people.

There needs to be much greater theoretical clarity on the question of a new curriculum. Many activists use the terms 'Afrocentric' and 'decolonised' interchangeably. Afrocentrism is a right-wing movement that emerged in the United States and is mostly closely associated with the conservative intellectual Molefi Asante. The decolonial movement is a radical movement that emerged in Latin America and is most closely associated with progressive intellectuals like Walter Mignolo and Enrique Dussel.

I also stressed that our universities are major national assets that need to be nurtured and to grow and develop into engines of social progress. I took a clear position that those who use intimidation, insult and character assassination are not radicals. The authentic radical project is rooted in democratic values and a commitment to rational discussion. There is no place for thuggery in our society – whether it comes from the police or students.

Now that the student movement has collapsed the hubris that often accompanied it seems rather silly. But the fundamental questions that drove the movement – coloniality, access and, at Rhodes, an end to rape and sexual harassment – remain absolutely urgent questions. With the benefit of hindsight, we can conclude that while the student movement made all kinds of serious mistakes it will go down in history as having raised three vital questions, two of which have significantly shifted national priorities in a manner that is fundamentally positive.

Universities have always been a site of social renewal. It is vital we invest in them. But as Ugandan scholar Mahmood Mamdani has shown, postcolonial states in Africa have tended to be deeply suspicious of universities precisely because they are where new ideas, and sometimes new political forces, emerge. Like most postcolonial governments, ours too has systemically underfunded universities. We all need to demand that universities be adequately funded. This is not solely a matter of resolving the material issues that have driven student protest. It is a matter of investing in ideas and the possibility of social and political renewal.

But the time of writing these reflections, Zuma's anti-intellectual patronage-driven project was giving way to what looks to be a return to technocratic rule under Cyril Ramaphosa's. Ramaphosa's desire to grow the economy will, logically, necessitate significant investment into universities and real attempts to broaden access. By the end of the Zuma era, there was widespread pessimism about the future of South African society in general, and universities were not spared from this. The future seemed exceedingly bleak. There is now a renewed optimism, and that optimism includes universities.

There can be no going back to the colonial curriculums that were largely unchallenged prior to 2015. There is a new danger, though, which is that the drive for economic competitiveness will mean that investment will largely be in the sciences. The humanities could find themselves in serious trouble. Already it is American foundations rather than a democratic state that dominate humanities funding.

There is a stone plaque at the entrance of the University of Dar es Salaam that reads: 'Those who receive this privilege therefore have a duty to repay the sacrifice which others have made. They are like the man who has been given all the food available in a starving village in order that he might have strength to bring supplies back from a distant place.'

The quote is from Mwalimu Julius Nyerere, first president of the

United Republic of Tanzania. He was speaking to students about the responsibility their privileged education brings. To whom much is given, much is expected. It's important that young people entering tertiary education heed his words.

The rise and fall of higher education costs: How 'free' is government's free education policy?

Zuko Godlimpi

THE DEBATE ON HIGHER education transformation in South Africa received a much-needed moral boost in 2015. For the first time in about 21 years, the more affluent campuses of UCT, Wits, Rhodes, Stellenbosch and the likes became the central axis around which progressive conversations were located about the structural setting of the higher education sector. There were two leading themes of this emerging discourse in 2015 and after: #RhodesMustFall and #FeesMustFall.

One centred around the racial power structures that underlie the culture, teaching and learning in mostly former white institutions, which was symbolised under the hashtag, #RhodesMustFall. Later on in the year the other leading theme, which became more popular, was the #FeesMustFall movement that addressed itself to the funding question in higher education.

Of course, there were overlapping sub-themes to both these main organising points. Both the #RhodesMustFall and #FeesMustFall campaigns directed attention to an elite framework of higher education. On the one hand they said exclusion manifests itself in the alienating cultural dynamics that privilege whiteness and white values (easily carried by English and Afrikaans as the only mediums of instruction) in education. Essentially, the philosophy of education in South Africa is rooted in a Eurocentric tradition that validates white experiences, recognises their systems of knowledge and procedures of knowing, while that philosophy invalidates the African experience, doesn't incorporate African values and rejects procedures of knowing that originate in African histories and systems of thought. The more academically inclined theoreticians refer to this philosophical tragedy of exclusion and forced assimilation as 'epistemic violence'.

On the other hand, the #FeesMustFall campaign exposed the effect of tertiary fees in enforcing a radicalised class power that privileges the rich – mostly white – to the exclusion of the poor, working class and mostly black students. 'If you cannot afford fees, you are not deserving of education.'

Thus, the point simultaneously made by RhodesMustFall and FeesMustFall is that the South African higher education sector is trapped in a crisis that interlocks race and class to exclude the majority of the country's population. In this intervention, I focus mainly on how university fees reinforce this crisis and whether the free education policy of government is a sufficient or near-sufficient response to unbundling this crisis.

The current government policy environment
On 16 December 2017 South Africa was greeted by news headlines reporting that President Jacob Zuma had released a statement announcing the introduction of free tertiary education. By this announcement the government of South Africa was transitioning from the loan-based National Students Financial Aid Scheme (NSFAS) that has been in operation since 1999, some 18 years ago.

In this regard, the announcement marked an important milestone in the more than 23 years of political agitation by progressive students' organisations for the introduction of free education, with varying government responses towards this outcome over the years. Since 1999 the democratic government has used reforms and improvements to the loan-based NSFAS as a platform for expanding access to higher education. Throughout this time, the scheme has been fraught with inadequacies in its funding that led to massive exclusions, increasing drop-out rates, growing institutional debt and a mounting student debt crisis that led to credit blacklisting among other things. It was not until 2009 that government finally put together a ministerial review committee to look at NSFAS with a view to produce a more sustainable higher education funding model for students. Professor Marcus Balintulo, the then vice chancellor of Walter Sisulu University, chaired this committee.

Importantly, the committee produced a comprehensive report by mid-2010, which outlined a number of recommended reforms to NSFAS. After its release, there was a conspicuous silence about the recommendations from government. However, its recommendations had an important bearing on the model proposed by government eight years later.

The 2017 Free Education policy announcement came two years after the popular #FeesMustFall protests of 2015, which was arguably the first mass protest against the costs of university and post-school education that gained support from the broadest spectrum of society and most notably the middle-class sections of South Africa. One of the reasons for this is that the rising costs of living in general, and by extension costs of higher education, have been increasingly catching up with relatively stagnant income levels. Thus, what were historically black, poor and working-class community struggles are increasingly becoming black middle-class struggles too!

Although the ruling ANC had acceded to political pressure from the progressive students' movement on this question, and by 2007 took a resolution to implement free education, its slow pace in translating that resolution to state policy produced the situation in which the #FeesMustFall moment appeared to be a decisive pressure point on government.

Thus, there is an urgent need for all progressive forces in society to reflect on the nature and substance of this policy intervention by government. Critical to these reflections is the question of whether or not the formulation of the policy reflects the strategic thrust of the free education demands by students over the last two decades.

A series of questions need to be posed and answered in order to gain a clearer picture of the operational understandings and misunderstandings of free education. What are the dominant conceptions of free education? What is the strategic justification for free education calls? Whose free education is this anyway? What are some competing approaches to state policy around funding free education that exist?

Whose free education is it?

There seems to be a widely held understanding that by free education students who enrol in higher education institutions will not be expected to pay fees. This has been the operational understanding of the student movement over the past two decades and it remained the same attitude of the #FeesMustFall campaigners. However, there is the less-stated point that in such a dispensation, fees would still exist, but students and their families they would no longer be directly paying them. The higher education system, including the enrolment fees of students, would have to be funded from elsewhere and most likely by the state.

In its policy announcement, the government impressed on all of us the understanding that it was not introducing a policy of 'universal free education'. Rather, this intervention was announced as a policy of fully subsidised education for students from poor and working-class backgrounds. This category of 'poor and working class' was defined as students from households with a combined income of less than R350 000 per annum. This means that all those whose combined household income is above this threshold will be required to pay fees in one way or another.

Firstly, the class appraisal of affordability is an opposite intervention. Although the strategic perspective is to ensure that all citizens gain access to institutions of knowledge acquisition, skills development and knowledge production, the necessary consideration of the means to afford remain crucial in order not to exempt from paying even the sections of society that are well off. State intervention in funding education must be pursued as an equity mechanism designed to provide access to those condemned to inability to pay as a consequence of racial and class inequality. Thus, the government position to ring fence this total subsidisation for the poor and working class, those who cannot afford, is a progressive consideration.

However, an important question arises on what frame of reference is used to determine the income bracket of those who can or cannot afford. Put differently, we may need to ask how it was determined that the category of 'poor and working class' corresponds to the income bracket of below R350 000 p/a in 2018. Was this an arbitrary income bracket or it was arrived at through some systematic calculation of average household costs against income? On its part, the government has not made any clarity regarding this categorisation. Yet, we have some historical context to arrive at a concerning conclusion about this.

In 2010 the Report of the Ministerial Review Committee on NSFAS recommended a three-tier student financial aid model.

The proposed higher education student financial aid scheme comprises three components aimed at different segments of the higher education student body, summarised as follows:

- Component 1: Full state subsidisation of poor students and those from working-class backgrounds, to be progressively realised over a specific period.
- Component 2: Income-contingent loan scheme for the children of public-sector employees earning salaries up to a maximum of R300 000 per annum.
- Component 3: Income-contingent loan scheme funded by the state or other agency for students from lower middle-income families.

The Ministerial Review Committee on NSFAS recommended free education for those who belonged to Component 1 and defined this component as those whose household income was below R150 000. At that time, it recommended an income-contingent loan scheme for Component 2 or 'the missing middle' or those whose combined household income was between R150 000 and R300 000.

In 2016 the government introduced a temporary subsidy that sought to cap fee increases in universities. The relief recognised that students from households whose combined household income was at R600 000 could not afford fee increases. This group was the one now being referred to as the 'missing middle'.

What we see here is that over a period of eight years these categories have shifted by 100%. Those who belonged to the 'missing middle' in 2010 are in 2017/18 firmly within the 'poor and working class'. Those who were arguably 'the rich' in 2010 appear in the 'missing middle' in government policy by 2017 income dynamics.

This 100% shift in these categories is driven by inflation dynamics that lead to a declining value of household income against rising costs of living. This is also compounded by the relatively autonomous inflation rate of university fees, which mostly rise at a rate that is higher than general consumer inflation. This autonomous inflation is also informed by the fact that universities independently determine fees and fee increments without a framework that imposes constraints. By this design, the rate of household income increase is far below the rate of inflation increase.

The ANC Youth League first drew the attention of government to this precarious nature of class categories in education policy formulation. In a statement released on 20 September 2016, responding to the announcement by the minister of higher education that there was a subsidy against fee increment for those whose household income of below R600 000, the ANCYL said:

> Whilst we welcome the concession that the working class and some middle-class income brackets cannot afford University fees and related increments, we believe that the intervention is missing the point. In the long term the sociology of the 'missing middle' is a 'moving target' that depends on the rate of general price inflation against the rate of increase in household income. Because increases in the rate of inflation tend to outpace increases in average household income, in a short time the 'missing middle' bracket will change.'

All of this leads us to the question: Is the below R350 000 bracket for free education an arbitrary categorisation of poor and working class? Is it an income bracket that is to be reviewed at the end of each year? Is ability to afford in terms of income brackets determined based on general consumer inflation trends or with due regard to autonomous higher education costs inflation? How will government keep track of the impact of fee increments on the shifting ability to afford if it cannot effectively predict the pace of higher education cost inflation?

In lieu of a conclusion
The introduction of free education or fully subsidised costs of education for the poor and working class is an important intervention. It will go a long way in improving access, reducing post-tertiary indebtedness of poor students and end the credit blacklisting that follows defaults on loan repayments. These are people who already carry a heavy intergenerational burden of pulling whole families out of poverty as soon as they gain employment.

However, the policy's substantive reach needs vigorous engagement by all stakeholders. The current model of relying on shifting class categories is unsustainable and does not fully cover the whole range of social groups that cannot afford to pay. It has only managed to reduce these social classes but has not eliminated them.

Moreover, there has been no direction on how government will regulate fee increments in general. Universities may use this policy intervention as a means to extort money from government by sustaining high rates of fee increments. The related crisis to this would be an increasing strain on state coffers as it would be funding a 'black hole' which it cannot reasonably budget for, given the fact that universities independently determine fees in the context of legislated institutional autonomy.

Can free education and wide-ranging higher education transformation be successfully conceived of within the context of institutional autonomy and academic freedom as currently legislated? Can the South African black middle class keep up with the rising costs of higher education? Is there no feasible way of introducing universal free education in public universities in a manner that shifts the costs to the rich and wealthy? These are all issues that need to be addressed for us to carry this debate forward.

The critical point of discussion that remains is about developing a sustainable funding model that extends benefits of free education to an increasing number of social classes. That funding model would still have to retain the principle of not exempting those who can afford to pay. Yet the discussion about who exactly can and cannot afford to pay, as a long-term categorisation, needs to be given serious attention.

Fees Must Fall: A holistic approach will stand us all in good stead

Oscar Van Heerden and Nicky Roberts

At the time of the first protest action of students from institutions of higher learning, we penned an open letter to the then minister of finance in which we cautioned that a short-sighted approach to this very real challenge will be folly. Instead, what will benefit us all in the long run will be a holistic approach to the challenge facing the entire education sector. That letter went as follows and remains relevant today still.

IN CONTRAST TO APPORTIONING blame to you Mr Minister, for the situation at the University of the Witwatersrand, we would like to thank you for the delicate balancing act which your department is performing. We would like to commend the South African government for maintaining the rule of law and upholding the autonomy of higher education institutions. We would like to further commend you for the work you and your department are doing to closely guard both how our public money is spent and ensure that income owing to our public purse reaches it.

We would like to thank you for responding to the under-funding of higher education relatively swiftly and for the additional funding which this sector has received last year (2016). We refer to the statement made by Minister Blade Nzimande:

1. Higher education and training this year received an additional

18% for 2016/17, with an average annual increase of 9.8% across the medium-term expenditure Framework period up until 2018/19. From R42 billion in the 2015/16 financial year, the Department's budget is set to rise to R55.3 billion in 2018/19.
2. Government has this year provided R1.9 billion of the R2.3 billion shortfalls resulting from the subsidisation of the 2016 university fee increase.
3. More than R4.5 billion in the 2016/17 financial year has been reprioritised to the National Student Financial Aid Scheme (NSFAS).

We support the call for additional funding for higher education and for putting education at the centre of our national agenda. In fact, we think this is in line with our collective 2030 vision, where education (which we take to mean life-long learning) is prioritised. We further support the calls for 'free education' (which we take to mean 'education that is not paid for by poor South Africans').

We know that education costs money and that quality education costs a lot. We know too that our education system is highly unequal and that there is a need to craft and wield pro-poor redress mechanisms at all levels of the system (from prenatal women's health of learners, not yet born, to the first thousand days of a learner's life to their second birthday, through early childhood development to primary and secondary schooling and finally into higher education). For while education is a weapon for emancipation, so too is it a weapon for social exclusion and economic marginalisation.

We do not agree that higher education ought to be the biggest priority within the public education spending and re-prioritisation of our national budget. While more higher education funding is needed, we do not think that this should all come from the public purse. We believe that universities are privileged, well-organised networks of advantaged individuals who ought to be encouraged to leverage their funding requirements from a range of sources. We certainly think that the South African private sector is able to invest more into these institutions.

We fear that the current demands by a small group of university students, at times supported by academic staff, are neither reasonable, nor attainable. We refer back to the historic texts which reflect education as one of our key national and public assets. The Freedom Charter stipulates that,

> The Doors of Learning and Culture Shall be Opened! The government shall discover, develop and encourage national talent for the enhancement of our cultural life; All the cultural treasures of mankind shall be open to all, by free exchange of books, ideas and contact with other lands; The aim of education shall be to teach the youth to love their people and their culture, to honour human brotherhood, liberty and peace; Education shall be free, compulsory, universal and equal for all children; Higher education and technical training shall be opened to all by means of state allowances and scholarships awarded on the basis of merit; Adult illiteracy shall be ended by a mass state education plan; Teachers shall have all the rights of other citizens; The colour bar in cultural life, in sport and in education shall be abolished.

The choice of words here, with education as 'free ... and equal for all children' (0–18-year-olds), was both significant and deliberate. 'Higher education open to all, by means of state allowances and scholarships', is a well-considered component of the county's vision of opening the doors of learning and culture.

Consulting the ANC resolution from the 2012 Mangaung conference reveals a similar policy commitment: 'Implementing free higher education for the poor in South Africa' and 'free higher education for all undergraduate level from poor and working-class communities for phase implementation from 2014'. The later parts of the higher education resolution also refer to 'academically capable students from poor families ...' and later to 'academically capable students from working class and lower middle class families...'

In a country that suffers from the triple concerns of poverty, inequality and lack of decent work, how the national budget is used to redress the past and create opportunities for the present is a very tough decision. As you know more than most, this requires balancing expenditure allocations for competing priorities, ensuring sufficient public income and also finding creative ways in which the public funds can be augmented from other sources.

We think the current government path of prioritising free higher education funding for the poor must be maintained. We therefore appeal to you to maintain the distinction between 'free education' and 'zero fees for all'. Fees are used as per-student levy, which can effect transformation and prioritise particular groups in society to experience 'free education'. In the absence of using fees as one possible redress mechanism, our fear is that the rich citizens (who earn more than R600 000 per annum) will no longer contribute to the higher education via fees but continue to take up available undergraduate places. There will be no fees for them to pay, and/or they will migrate to private higher education institutions, and/or they will access higher education in foreign countries. Our public higher education institutions cannot benefit from this potential source of non-government funding. With 'zero fees' our universities will not obtain the fee income from foreign governments who send their students to our public institutions; or private companies that pay for priority qualifications.

We know that some of our academic colleagues, students and friends will label us as reactionary, ANC/government-apologists, counter-revolutionary, liberal, neo-liberal, racist, conservative, neo-conservative, anti-liberation, colonial relics and anti-student. So be it.

We choose to defend ourselves here on just one of these labels (anti-student). The 'students', for whom we may appear to be 'anti-student', are not the 'students' to which we refer. You see – unlike our colleague who wrote to you earlier – we don't work only with undergraduate students. In particular, Nicky's work is much lower down in the education hierarchy, which also desperately requires fixing and investment to make us the nation we hope for. So 'the students' we hold in mind are different to those whom Dr Gillespie chooses to describe to you.

The students we hold in mind are the poor South African and SADC students at our universities who face very serious hardship of not completing this year.

The students we hold in mind are the 5–6-year-olds who had a chance of being offered a second year of free education at pre-Grade R level. This major investment now seems very less likely.

We hold in mind the students between the ages of zero and five for whom there is very little 'free education' at all. This is a time in their life that we know has the most impact on their future, and at a point in time when we know we get the best return on investment in terms of learning outcomes and the possibility for future learning. Unlike at undergraduate levels, where throughputs are only one in three, investing early in education for the poor has been shown internationally to yield far greater results. The students we hold in mind are the students at TVET colleges and historically disadvantaged universities who sacrificed their pro-poor state infrastructure grants to increase state spending on undergraduate funding for all.

We are also aware that both the undergraduates burning and throwing stones as well as those who are casualties caught in the cross fire of these protests are a small minority of our South African university students, who in turn are a very small minority (only 12%) of their Grade 1 class who started formal schooling with them.

The students we hold in mind are the students in-utero in poor communities, whose mothers don't yet access paltry child grants (which are R4 200 a year in comparison to R8 113.50 which our colleague Professor Vally reports is the current government expenditure on an undergraduate student at Wits). These young students require micro-nutrients, food, safety, protection from violence and other basic human rights to provide a stable and loving home where toxic stress is reduced, so that their brain architecture for all future learning can develop healthily.

We draw on both brain science and economics for our argument to support early investment in education for all of South Africa's poor. On a more personal note, we simply cannot justify not paying for our children's higher education and so contributing directly to the higher education pie. Nicky knows how much she benefited from the state investments, which furthered her white privilege. We both know we cannot be South African graduates, using our degrees to get a job (placing us in this rich category) and not pay directly towards higher education. Either we pay for our children's education or we contribute to a graduate tax, or both.

Please, please, please consider the smoke and noise from whence it comes. When decisions are made that gloss over the lived experiences of inequality, and claim that 'all lives matter', or 'all animals are equal' or 'free education for all' (and especially when these are shouted with revolutionary fervour from the ivory towers of certain universities), we inadvertently get greater inequality: a situation we simply cannot support. We cannot defend nor justify a situation where a privileged few who shout the loudest to ensure they are first in line to thrust a begging bowl at our National Treasury, get to eat more of the pie.

You know that South Africa is a far bigger society than its universities. We appeal for greater public investments in women's health, pre-natal care, programmes and economic support for parents of young children, free ECD education in our poor communities and greater efficiency and repayment rates from NSFAS before more of our money is directed to the university level to service those who are far better placed to access funding from non-government sources than the rest of our poor and less educated citizens are.

Contributors' biographies

Adam Buch was a student journalist studying for his honours in development studies at the University of Cape Town in 2015. Adam is currently doing an MA in development studies and hopes to complete another in public health. He is the founder and editor-in-chief of Making a Difference, an online platform to fight for good ideas.

Akhona Mdunge is a law student at the University of Pretoria. He is an active member, and the current secretary-general, of the Democratic Alliance Student Organisation, University of Pretoria branch. He is currently serving as the study finances official in the university's student representative council. Akhona was born in Durban and was raised in Pinetown in KwaZulu-Natal. He attended St Benedict School where he served as the head boy in 2015.

Anele Madonsela is a former student activist born in KwaZulu-Natal. She came to Johannesburg to begin her studies double majoring in psychology and philosophy at the University of Johannesburg in 2014. She was expelled from the University of Johannesburg in 2016 for her involvement in #UJFeesMustFall and campus shutdowns.

Annabel Fenton is a graduate from the University of Cape Town and a youth policy activist passionate about combining on-the-ground collaboration, policymaking and academic experience to formulate creative and inclusive solutions to sustainable development in Africa. She is an Allan Gray Orbis Foundation Candidate Fellow doing her geography postgraduate research at the University of the Witwatersrand. In 2014 Annabel was a South African delegate at the international G(irls)20 Summit.

Asanda Luwaca is currently employed as a researcher in the African National Congress (ANC) Parliamentary Caucus. Before working in Parliament, she was employed as an assistant researcher at the Mapungubwe Institute for Strategic Reflection (MISTRA). She holds a bachelor's degree in politics and is pursuing her postgraduate degree in political science at the University of South Africa.

Azola Dayile is a writer from Kwazakhele, Port Elizabeth. He studied journalism, media and philosophy at the Nelson Mandela University (NMU). In 2014, together with other students, he formed a radical student collective, the Black Students Stokvel to drive the decolonial agenda and push for free education at NMU. In the wake of the 2015/16 #FeesMustFall student movement, Azola formed an integral part, making links with student/worker activists in the country and elsewhere. He currently lives in Joburg where he thinks and writes for a living.

Busani Ngcaweni is Head of Policy and Research Services in the Presidency and Non-Resident Research Fellow at the University of Johannesburg. He has edited volumes such as *The Future We Chose: Emerging Perspectives on the Centenary of the ANC* (AISA, 2013), *Liberation Diaries: Reflections on 20 Years of Democracy in South Africa* (Jacana Media, 2014), *Sizonqoba: Outliving AIDS in Southern Africa* (AISA, 2016) and *Nelson R Mandela: Decolonial Ethics of Liberation and Servant Leadership* (Africa World Press, 2018) with Sabelo Ndlovu-Gatsheni. He contributes articles in various news outlets like the *Daily Maverick*.

David Maimela, a master's student at the University of Johannesburg, is the former political economy researcher at the Mapungubwe Institute for Strategic Reflection (MISTRA). Maimela is also a former president of SASCO and remains active in the progressive youth movement. He is currently the chief of staff in the Office of the Competition Commissioner.

Enhle Lucinda Khumalo is an avid reader and a social strategist and community manager. Enhle has a Bachelor of Arts (Honours) in international relations and holds a master's degree in political studies from the University of the Witwatersrand. She does freelance writing and is the founder of MbalEnhlesis, an African-inspired brand with a social conscious. In previous years she has served as the deputy junior mayor of Johannesburg and as the research and policy officer for the Wits SRC.

Gugu Ndima has served as the national spokesperson of the Young Communist League and continues to serve as an active member of the ANC Youth League. She has served as a media and communications officer in the Office of the Chief Whip of the ANC in the Gauteng Legislature and worked as spokesperson to the Speaker of the Legislature. Her self-published fiction book, *All in a Gal'z Life*, will be republished in 2019 and soon followed by her second novel, *Ntombenhle*. Her articles have appeared in the *Sunday Independent* and the *Sowetan*. Ndima is studying law at the University of Johannesburg.

Imraan Buccus is a research fellow in the School of Social Sciences at the University of KwaZulu-Natal. He is a newspaper columnist and political analyst on TV news agencies. He is widely published in academic journals and book chapters in the areas of participatory democracy, poverty and civil society.

Jordan Pfotenhauer is an LLB final-year student at the University of Cape Town. He is the Western Cape Schools Debating Board (WCSDB) other chief adjudicator for 2017/2018. He previously served as the chairperson of the UCT Debating Society over the 2015/2016 period.

Kgaugelo Sebidi is a Rhodes Scholar reading for an MPhil in development studies at the University of Oxford. Prior to Oxford, he was a junior researcher at the Human Sciences Research Council in Cape Town. He holds a BA honours degree in development studies and a bachelor's degree in psychology from the University of Cape Town and the University of Johannesburg, respectively. His current research focuses on higher education transformation in South Africa and comparatively explores the conceptualisations of 'Transformation' in historically black and historically white universities.

Khanyisile Melanie Mboya was a negotiator during the #FeesMustFall movement in 2015 at Rhodes University and a key mediator in 2016. She graduated in 2016 from the University Currently Known as Rhodes simultaneously with her bachelor and honours degrees in industrial and economic sociology at the age of 22.

Kneo Mokgopa is a young editor and writer at the University of Cape Town law school. He is known for poetry and performance after representing South Africa at the Brave New Voices international poetry festival in 2013. Kneo is the editor-in-chief of *The Africxn Magazine*, the African Union Chapter's bi-annual fine art and literary journal publication; current affairs senior at Altum Sonatur, UCT law school's journal publication; as well as an independent artist producing photographic essays on abstracting and reimagining gender.

Lovelyn Nwadeyi is a young and vibrant Nigerian–South African woman who hails from Queenstown in the Eastern Cape. She holds a BA international studies degree from Stellenbosch University and an MSc Peace and Conflict Studies degree from Uppsala University in Sweden. She has been involved in diverse roles related to student and worker activism during the first wave (2015) of the movements of #FeesMustFall and #EndOutsourcing in South Africa. Lovelyn regularly speaks on matters related to the decolonisation of education, socio-economic justice and gender justice.

Mabone Lerato Kgosiemang is a PhD candidate in the sociology department at the University of Johannesburg. He has an MA in social impact assessment and an honours in public management and governance all from the University of Johannesburg. Mabone is a student activist and community activist with interests in student politics and race.

Mcebo Freedom Dlamini is a law student and graduate from the University of the Witwatersrand. Mcebo is a former student representative council chairperson at Wits and a key student leader at Wits during the Fees Must Fall movement between 2015 to 2016. He continues to be a student activist.

Natasha Ndlebe is a language practice graduate from Tshwane University of Technology. She is a writer who is passionate about editing. Despite her introverted spirit, she enjoys debating and defying aspects considered the norm.

Nicky Roberts is an associate professor at the University of Johannesburg's Centre for Education Practice Research. Her academic focus is on a narrative approach to learning during childhood with a particular focus on a narrative approach to mathematics.

Nkateko Mabasa is a Johannesburg-based writer and journalist at the *Daily Maverick* and an avid reader of African literature who believes art is not for art's sake but to serve humanity. In literature, we not only find ourselves but he believes in the inspiration to invent the future.

Nkhensani Manabe is a writer and editor based in Johannesburg. She has an undergraduate degree in media and writing from the University of Cape Town and an honours degree in publishing studies from the University of the Witwatersrand. Her interests include anything that concerns the representation of women in film, television and literature in Africa and the diaspora, feminism and digital content creation.

Ntokozo Qwabe is a South African Rhodes Scholar who was one of the founders of the Rhodes Must Fall campaign at Oxford University. Qwabe was also one of the founders of the Rhodes Must Fall campaign which originated at the University of Cape Town in South Africa and was originally directed at a statue of Cecil Rhodes.

Oscar Van Heerden is a scholar of international relations (IR), who focuses on the international political economy with an emphasis on Africa and the ADC in particular. He completed his PhD and master's studies at the University of Cambridge. His undergraduate studies were at Turfloop and Wits. He is an active fellow of the Mapungubwe Institute for Strategic Reflections (MISTRA) and is a trustee for the Kgalema Motlanthe Foundation

Qhama Bona holds a Bachelor of Arts undergraduate degree in sociology and political science and an honours degree in political science. He obtained both degrees at the Nelson Mandela University in Port Elizabeth. He is a community activist in East London and is Interim Secretary for an NGO in East London called Kwanele People's Movement.

Ramabina Mahapa served as the student representative council president of the University of Cape Town in 2015. He holds a bachelor's degree majoring in psychology and philosophy from UCT and an honours degree in African Studies, with distinction, from the same institution.

Robert Nkuna is Director-General of the Department of

Telecommunications and Postal Services since 2016. Prior to that he was Advisor to Minister Ben Martins at the Departments of Transport and Energy. He has served terms as Councillor at the Independent Communications Authority of SA (ICASA) and was Board Member at the Media Development and Diversity Agency (MDDA). Nkuna was a student activist who led campus-based and national structures in SASCO and the SA Students Press Union.

Rofhiwa Maneta is a Cape Town-based writer, photographer and self-published author. He has previously been published by *Mail & Guardian*, VICE and OkayAfrica.

Sabelo J. Ndlovu-Gatsheni is a professor and head of Archie Mafeje Research Institute for Applied Social Policy based at the University of South Africa. He is also the founder and coordinator of the Africa Decolonial Research Network (ADERN) based in the College of Human Sciences at the University of South Africa. He has published many papers and books on decolonisation.

Sarah Mokwebo is a graduate and postgraduate student from the University of the Witwatersrand. She was a student leader during the Fees Must Fall movement. She is a feminist activist whose interests are on debunking patriarchy and centring intersectionality.

Sibusiso Chalufu is the dean of students at the University of South Africa (UNISA) and the deputy president of the Southern African Federation of Student Affairs and Services in Higher Education (SAFSAS). He also serves on the Universities South Africa's (USAf) Transformation Strategy Group and on the DHET's Reference Group on Student Funding Policy. During the Fees Must Fall period he was Executive Director: Student Services at the University of KwaZulu-Natal (UKZN).

Sisonke Msimang is a South African writer whose work is focused on race, gender and democracy. She has written for a range of international publications including the *New York Times*, the *Guardian*, *Newsweek* and Al Jazeera. Her first book, *Always Another Country: A Memoir of Exile and Home*, was published in South Africa in October 2017.

Tshepiso Modupe hails from a Bodibe village in North West province. A former first-year clinical medicine student at Wits, she is currently studying towards a degree in politics at North-West University.

Tlhabane Dan Motaung is a senior researcher in the faculty of humanities at the Mapungubwe Institute for Strategic Reflection (MISTRA). He was a student leader at the Witwatersrand university in the mid-90s.

Wandile Ngcaweni is a junior researcher at the Mapungubwe Institute for Strategic Reflection (MISTRA). He holds a degree in development studies from the University of Johannesburg and is currently completing his honours in development studies at the University of South Africa. He was part of the Fees Must Fall protests at the University of Johannesburg in 2016. He has attended the Decolonial Summer School at UNISA and is an alumni of the Thabo Mbeki African Leadership Institute. He writes opinion pieces for various newspapers.

Zuko Godlimpi is a member of the ANC Youth League and works as a researcher in the local government sphere. A free-thinking youth activist, he contributes articles in newspapers and is a social media blogger.